Forest energy and economic development

Forest energy and economic development

D. E. EARL

CLARENDON PRESS · OXFORD
1975

Oxford University Press, Ely House, London W. 1

GLASGOW NEW YORK TORONTO MELBOURNE WELLINGTON
CAPE TOWN IBADAN NAIROBI DAR ES SALAAM LUSAKA ADDIS ABABA
DELHI BOMBAY CALCUTTA MADRAS KARACHI LAHORE DACCA
KUALA LUMPUR SINGAPORE HONG KONG TOKYO

ISBN 0 19 854521 5

© Oxford University Press 1975

Printed in Great Britain
by J. W. Arrowsmith Ltd., Bristol

Preface and Acknowledgements

The sharp price increases of fuels and all tradeable goods in 1973–4, sparked off by the oil producers' exercise of their monopolistic might, comes as a timely warning of the likely effect on the world economy of a predicted general shortage of hitherto easily-obtainable fossil fuels. Increasing supplies of energy are needed to maintain a basic standard of living for a rapidly expanding world population and for economic growth but it is known that coal, gas, and oil reserves cannot continue indefinitely to meet the major part of the world's energy needs. The forecasted economic crisis, if allowed to develop, will have severe repercussions upon the developing world in its struggle to raise living standards and will shake the structure of the affluent society to its foundations.

It is believed by many economists who are unfamiliar with the Second Law of Thermodynamics (the Entropy Law), and are unwilling to differentiate between renewable and non-renewable resources, that the price mechanism will enable technology to produce enough energy from nuclear fission, or fusion, or some other source as yet unknown, to meet the predicted future energy requirements. The snags with power production from nuclear fission are that it is dependent upon the existence of uranium, a diminishing resource, and its use has many disadvantages, including the difficulty of storing highly dangerous radioactive waste products. The use of energy from nuclear fusion depends upon the emergence of technologies capable of coping with the problem of controlling the reactions and because such control may never become possible on a large scale, the belief that it will provide the panacea for economic ills is, to a large extent, wishful thinking.

The most serious aspect of relying upon economic forces and technology to solve the growing energy problem is the danger that mankind may be led into the trap of having to make decisions under crisis conditions, and without well-defined ecological constraints to economic activity, deterioration and, ultimately, destruction of the biosphere may ensue.

It is not imperative to develop vast supplies of nuclear energy for mankind's survival as has been suggested by some authorities, for renewable sources of energy offer a safer and environmentally more satisfactory solution to the long-term energy supply problem and taken together with a prudent population policy the renewable sources of fuel and power, if well planned and fully developed, could provide for all the energy needs of the world. Renewable power is produced principally from hydro-electric, geothermal, tidal, and direct solar sources and renewable fuel is produced from the chemical combination of carbon dioxide and water by plants with the aid of solar energy in photosynthesis. The carefully-controlled use of nuclear power would then be needed only for special purposes where very high temperatures were required and fossil fuel resources would be used mainly as chemical feedstocks where comparative advantage exists, for example, for providing plastics and fertilizers, and only rarely burnt in power stations, domestic boilers, and transport systems.

If the thesis is accepted, how practical is the gradual replacement of energy from fossil fuel by supplies from renewable sources? Evidence shows that this is feasible and immediately acceptable economically and socially in those countries with low population densities and adequate forests. The reserve of energy held by forests is more than twenty times greater than the world's current annual consumption of energy from all sources and the world's forests incorporate solar energy into organic material, from which can be obtained solid, liquid, and gaseous fuels, at an annual rate far in excess of the world's present economic needs.

The biggest reserve of renewable fuel is in the tropical countries, where the forests have the greatest capacity for regeneration. Unfortunately, the destruction of tropical forests in developing countries is accelerated as soon as economic growth is initiated. One of the tragedies of the time is that the real needs of the people who live there are often ignored until it is too late. The developing world depends on fuelwood to supply 90 per cent of its energy needs but the people themselves do not realize the extent of the ecological damage done because, for them, wood has been an abundant social good; and it is therefore only by the institution of suitably-planned economic growth based upon the realization of the value of their indigenous renewable fuel resources that forests can be saved. If energy as a component of the many benefits obtainable from mixed forests and from energy plantations is to become an effective part of the world's energy budget in future, the forest policies of many countries must be adjusted so as to fulfil this role. The present pattern of economic growth, which has no ecological basis, is likely to exacerbate the energy problem. Development goals based on the net long-term benefit criterion must be established to ensure that the forest and the soil are able to provide man with the basic needs of fuel and food. Planning must be instituted to ensure that land and resources are not sacrificed to short-term objectives.

There are books devoted to the study of forests as providers of timber, and others that deal with the chemical and physical properties of timber but to my knowledge none so far has attempted an holistic assessment of forests as major stores and suppliers of energy. The potential of this vast reservoir of energy is placed in perspective and the means by which it can be managed to ensure its continuity are discussed. It is hoped that in addition to providing practical help to foresters, this book will be of value to economists, planners, and sociologists working in the disparate sectors of all economies.

I owe a very great debt of gratitude to the many people who have encouraged me with useful ideas and constructive criticism over the past ten years. I would like to acknowledge the help received from my colleagues in the Uganda Forest Department and in particular Mr. M. L. S. B. Rukuba, who helped me to develop a sound silvicultural method of treating tropical forests in the most cost-effective way so as to provide fuel and timber without the use of arboricides. Also deserving of my gratitude are the staff of the Department of Forestry and the Commonwealth Forestry Institute at Oxford; the Forestry Section of the Food and Agriculture Organization of the United Nations for providing much of the basic material from which I have constructed my thesis, and the Forestry Commission.

Among those individuals who have given me constant support at the Department of Forestry, Oxford, are: Mr. J. J. MacGregor, who has been a fountain of valuable suggestions made with a combination of intellectual ability, tact, and good humour rarely found together in such measure; Dr. W. R. C. Handley, who has always stressed the need to balance the economic and social importance of forests against the necessity for caring for the land resource in order that the production of biological material can be maintained; and my companions in the Forest Economics Research Room, especially Mr. C. Price, who have through many discussions and seminars served to remind me throughout that a critical approach to every idea, especially one's own, is essential if any real progress is to be made.

Finally I wish to record the very special debt which I owe to my wife, who has offered much constructive criticism of the text and has tackled the onerous task of typing many drafts with cheerful willingness. Without her help this book would never have reached the Press.

Oxford   D. E. E.
August 1974

Contents

List of Plates

1 Economic growth, development, and energy

'Nature has bestowed upon us an inquisitive
disposition . . . Our vision opens up a path
for its investigation and lays the foundation
of truth so that our research may pass from
revealed to hidden things.'
Seneca, *On leisure*

Productive processes depend upon the availability of land, capital, and labour.
Social costs and benefits feature much more than hitherto in the analysis of economic growth and because energy is a capital resource common to all processes, a
study of forest energy cannot be carried out in isolation from the wider issues
involved.

Economic growth

It is widely agreed that greater economic activity, resulting in an increased gross
national product (GNP), is desirable, but only comparatively recently has it become generally accepted that unrestricted economic growth may have external
effects which nullify most, if not all, of the advantages gained. It is therefore
incumbent upon those who seek to encourage economic growth to understand
the special problems that may arise from its promotion.

The material progress of a nation is usually estimated by measuring the change
in GNP per annum. Occasionally gross domestic product (GDP) is used as this
excludes earnings from overseas investment. The GNP criterion has been much
criticized by Galbraith (1969) who suggests that its use as a yardstick for the
measurement of growth is retrogressive if 'net real growth' is required. In particular he has laid stress on its inability to measure diseconomies such as the
increased pollution associated with industrial progress.

The effect of economic growth upon the quality of life and the environment
has been the subject of much recent controversy. Beckerman (1972a) believes
that economic theory can identify and also indicate solutions to the pollution
problem and that a balance has to be struck between the protection of the environment and the use of resources. The social optimum does not require that
pollution should be completely eliminated for some pollution is inevitable; and,
by the principle of 'the polluter pays', externalities may be 'internalized'. He
postulates that the discount rate forms part of a well-defined analytical framework

for dealing with future pollution and that there is no conflict between economic growth and preservation of the environment. Growth is at the expense of consumption foregone and therefore the problem is between the allocation of resources used today or in the future. Although present consumption may lead to environmental deterioration, all the major features of the environmental problem can be greatly clarified in the light of existing economic theory. In another article, Beckerman (1972b) makes a swingeing attack on 'eco-doomsters' and the 'limits-to-growth school' who say that because E (ecological demand) $\equiv f$ (GDP) it is therefore logical to stop GDP in order to halt an indefinite rise in E. Economists are interested in phenomena only as they affect human beings and prefer to look at possible changes in f; exponential growth in demand for a finite resource has existed from the beginning and did not prevent economic growth from taking place. Similarly the contention by Meadows, Meadows, Randers, and Behrens (1972) that economic growth has led to increasing inequality of income distribution, including an increasing gap between the rich and poor countries, proves nothing, as inequality has existed since time began.

The World Bank each year publishes an atlas in which the GNP *per capita* of all countries in the world are shown. The publishers qualify the usefulness of the figures given by drawing attention to the following points. Figures for GNP are in many instances based upon data that are approximate at best; their conversion to U.S. dollars introduces yet another source of error. The use of exchange rates for the conversion of currencies may result in a considerable over-statement of product differences among countries, especially as between those in the highest and lowest income categories.

A study carried out in India in 1959 by the World Bank indicated that whereas at current exchange rates the U.S.A. *per capita* product exceeded that of India by a ratio of 30 : 1, a purchasing power parity calculation yielded a ratio of approximately 12 : 1. The reason for this lies primarily in the divergent price and product structure of the different countries. Exchange rates, even when they approximate balance-of-payment equilibrium rates, equate at best the prices of internationally-traded goods and services only. They may bear little relationship to the goods and services not entering international trade, which, in most developing countries, form the bulk of the national product. Agricultural products and services in particular are generally priced lower in relation to industrial output in developing than in industrialized countries—and agriculture typically accounts for much the largest share of total product in the developing countries. The result is that the currency conversion method used tends to exaggerate the real income differences between less-developed and more-developed countries.

The use of exchange rates for converting national currency estimates into U.S. dollar equivalents is further complicated by the fact that the official or par-value rates do not always constitute equilibrium rates. Countries experiencing substantial inflation frequently maintain pegged exchange rates over long periods, so that a straight conversion on the basis of the over-valued rates would overstate both the absolute level of the GNP in terms of U.S. dollars and its increase over time.

Provided that the limitations to their use are understood, GNP *per capita* criteria are useful as very rough indicators of national income and helpful in measuring the material economic progress of societies. They highlight the tremendous inequalities in wealth that exist between nations, and emphasize the need for an increasing world commitment to assist the developing countries in their efforts to improve the conditions of life of their peoples. The writer thinks that economic growth is desirable provided it is controlled so that it leads to the long-term enrichment of the lives of people generally. An understanding of what is meant by desirable economic growth is necessary before undertaking to explain why the forest energy resource has an important if not vital role to play in the development process.

Development

The economic rationale of development is that scarce resources should be utilized so as to maximize the net long-term social benefits for mankind. In order to achieve a social end, development requires the selection of material and social goals such as the reduction in poverty and the greater equality of income. GNP can grow without any improvement in these socially critical areas and is, therefore, by itself not an adequate measure of development and although to some extent the selection of social goals is left to politicians in each country, the compilation of a set of social indicators which can be applied to all the economies of the world is of international concern.

Whatever views may be held upon development, it is clear that most people, particularly those in developing countries, associate it with growth of national product and that despite the externalities, economic growth is what they want, hence the large-scale migration to conurbations which has taken place and continues to take place throughout the world. The real income *per capita* criterion will continue to be considered as playing a dominant role in determining the progress of development particularly for those at the income levels where the marginal utility of money is at its highest and, to be realistic, very few social indicators can show an advance unless there is an increase in the tax base recoverable from a rising GNP of a country.

The initiation of development

Everyone is aware that, in material terms, there is a vast gap between the people of the poorest and richest nations. The economies of these two groups are rather euphemistically described as developing and developed[†]. It may be invidious to postulate at which precise point a country changes status from developing to developed, but in material terms and as a rough guide only, those countries with

---

† Developing countries may be highly developed from the moral, cultural, and religious standpoints, but because they have not experienced any of the four revolutions—industrial, agricultural, health, and birth-control—that are familiar to Western countries, they are consequently still poor; Political and Economic Planning (1955).

GNP *per capita* below U.S. $500 per annum are assumed, in the context of this book, to be developing and those with GNP *per capita* above U.S. $1000 per annum are considered as being developed.

A major problem is how to reduce the gap which exists between developing and developed countries. Although parity may be the political aim of developing countries, a more realistic aim would be the achievement of a minimum subsistence level of nutrition and a basic education as a prerequisite to further progress. Poverty is an emotive word which has meaning only in relative terms but its removal is a main aim of development. Analysis of developing regions discloses some characteristics common to most of them:

low GNP;

low tax base;

high population growth;

low developed resource base;

shortage of entrepreneurial skills;

abundant and under-utilized man-power reserves; and

undeveloped land resources including natural forests.

It is sometimes assumed that economically poor countries should strive to emulate the richer, more advanced countries which have passed through the poor developing stage themselves before reaching a richer developed stage, which is, by presumption, the desired end of human achievement.

Economists concerned with development in developing countries do not believe that each country passes through comparable stages of growth. It is pointed out by Streeten (1967), in a discussion of the main factors affecting the development process now, as compared with those which prevailed in earlier times, that the co-existence of rich and poor countries alters the prospects of the poor countries for various reasons: the benefits of aid and knowledge to developing countries from countries already developed are well known but there are drawbacks which are less obvious. According to Streeten (1972) the slow growth rate in 'developing countries is caused by the 'technology gap' which may be attributable to imperfections in communicating and transferring existing technologies (i.e. 'communications gap'), or the absence of appropriate technologies (i.e. 'suitability gap'). The transfer of technology from developed economies to developing countries is often basically inappropriate because of different ratios of capital and sophisticated skills to unskilled labour, and furthermore imported technology usually depends upon large-scale production processes which, even with the best communications, poor countries simply do not have the resources to maintain. Compared with rich countries, poor countries have to provide about three times the number of jobs with about one-twentieth of the investable resources per worker.

There is a bias towards investment in urban development in developing countries noted by Lipton and Streeten (1968) who refer to India, where the rural sector with 70 per cent of the workers gets less than 35 per cent of investment finance and a far smaller share of human skills. This bias is not confined to developing economies but this is not to say that it should not be recognized and attempts made to avoid it.

One of the biggest factors inhibiting development in Africa is lack of entrepreneurship. Marris (1968) made a survey of fifty small industrial enterprises all of which had received loans from the Industrial and Commercial Development Corporation of Kenya. He came to the conclusion that although africanization is comparatively simple as it depends upon training Africans to replace foreigners in activities and organizations already established, the encouragement of entrepreneurship requires more originality and initiative. He suggests that without the latter it is doubtful whether African society can acquire any economic vitality. Neither the resources of money or skill nor the nature of society seem crucial determinants of their progress or talent. The distinctive quality of entrepreneurship is not the ability to run a business, invent techniques, or persuade customers to buy, nor the ability to forecast and profit by economic trends. It is a very original and very practical perceptiveness—an ability to assemble or reassemble a new kind of activity from what is available, to re-interpret the meaning of things and fit them together in new ways. It is also a very concrete kind of imagination, alert to the specific opportunities of a particular place at a particular time, improvising from what lies to hand. Social segregation may be one of the most serious obstacles to the development of African enterprise. Government help may inhibit the evolution of a truly integrated economic relationship. Entrepreneurship must depend very greatly on the participants' range of experience and relationship.

The influence of corruption in public service is much more evident in developing economies and has been emphasized as playing a counter-productive role in the so called 'soft state', Myrdal (1968). In a later work, Myrdal (1970) goes further than anyone else to stress the need for social discipline in developing countries which is signified by deficiencies in their legislation and, in particular, in law observance and enforcement. There is a lack of obedience to rules and directives handed down to public officials at various levels, and collusion of these officials with powerful persons or groups of persons whose conduct they should regulate, and, at bottom, a general inclination of people in all strata to resist public controls and their implementation. Within the concept of the 'soft state' corruption is a phenomenon which seems to be generally on the increase in all countries, both developing and developed.

The view that economic growth can be handled by market forces, and benefits left for government to distribute by way of taxes, may be reasonable in developed countries but is open to suspicion in developing economies for a number of reasons listed well by Lipton (1970). The chief snag is that taxes are hard to pay, collect, and administer; both taxes and transfers are open to corruption because the country is poor, the tax payments low and the civil servants underpaid. In agricultural stabilization policies in poor countries the most productive course of action has to be abandoned because distributional effects must be considered; optimization cannot be achieved by redistribution of taxes.

The World Bank now considers that aid for developing countries should be geared to projects which aim at greater employment and greater equality of income distribution.

Until the mid-sixties it was often assumed by economic planners that forced industrialization via import-substitution was the main way in which economic development was to be promoted, but recent studies (Little, Scitovsky, and Scott 1970) have shown the significant distortion of the general economic structure which can be caused by import-substituting industrialization taking place behind high protective barriers. The tendency now is to encourage the growth of agriculture and forest industries which are based on indigenous resources.

Energy

Although it is generally recognized that energy is needed for economic growth, it has not been so widely appreciated that the economic process itself is governed by the energy laws. It is because of this central role of energy that knowledge of the First and Second Laws of Thermodynamics should contribute towards a better understanding of economic development. An understanding of the Second Law in particular, sometimes termed the Entropy Law, is essential to an appreciation of the economic difficulties facing over-developed societies and of the problems of initiating economic growth in developing countries.

The rapid rise in economic activity and the decline in the percentage of renewable energy utilized as more communities change from domestic to market economies are giving cause for concern to those who consider that the energy laws and ecological principles should have an influence upon economic planning.

Fig. 1.1 provides evidence of a very strong correlation between energy consumption and GNP which explains why the annual *per capita* consumption of energy in the developed is many times greater than that of the developing world.

The U.N. statistics of energy used *per capita* may give misleading impressions of the stage of economic progress reached because fuelwood and charcoal are usually excluded from published data. *The statistical yearbook 1971* (U.N. 1973) does not include the available figures of fuelwood consumption despite the fact that the world consumption of energy from fuelwood is greater than that from combined hydro-electric schemes, nuclear power, and geothermal sources which are all included. The forest energy consumed in kilograms of coal equivalent (CE) *per capita* has been calculated from recorded removal of fuelwood for selected countries and included in Table 1.1. From this table it can be ascertained that Nepal obtains 95·8 per cent of the energy requirement from forest sources whereas more than 90 per cent of the energy used in the U.S.A. comes from finite resources. This makes a very significant alteration to the actual relative *per capita* consumption between the U.S.A. and Nepal, which instead of 10 774 and 11 kilograms of CE, i.e. 979 : 1 (U.N. 1973) is shown to be 10 817 and 259 kilograms of CE, i.e. 42 : 1.

Fig. 1.2 illustrates the point that most of the non-forest energy is used by the developed world. Developing countries use more forest energy as an essential part

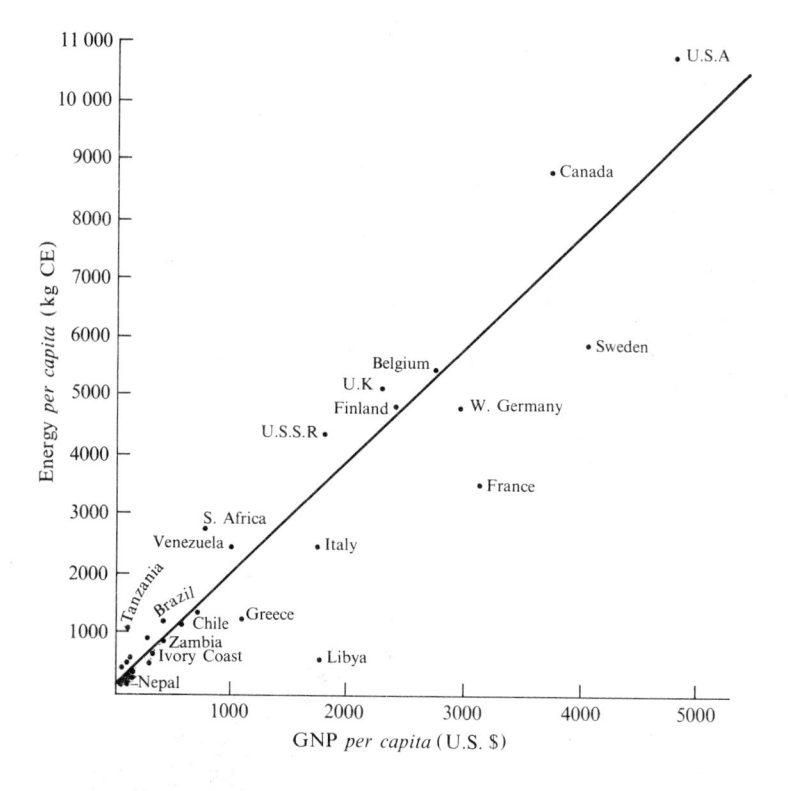

Fig. 1.1. Relationship between energy consumption and GNP for selected countries 1970.

of their economies than the developed countries but the value of this non-tradeable commodity is not used in the calculation of GNP *per capita*, which consequently undervalues the real standard of economic growth reached in developing countries.

The future for energy and economic growth

Domestic economies in many parts of the developing world rely upon renewable sources of energy to meet their needs. Developed countries have come to rely upon increasing consumption of finite fuel resources to maintain and increase their relative position in the world economy. The rationale for growth based upon the utilization of under-priced, non-renewable resources is now being challenged because it inevitably must result in irreversible depletion of the world's stock of finite energy in accordance with the dictates of the Entropy Law.

There should be much better control over fuel and power resources, for although energy consumption may not necessarily lead to development in the sense of improvement of society, energy is the key factor in the achievement of

Fig. 1.2. Energy consumption kg CE per capita 1970.

Non-forest sources > 1000
Non-forest and forest sources combined > 1000
Non-forest and forest sources combined < 1000

TABLE 1.1

Per capita GNP and energy consumption for some selected countries

Country	GNP per capita (US $)	Consumption per capita fuelwood (m³)	Energy consumption per capita (kg CE)† Forest only	Total	Proportion of total energy supplied by fuelwood (%)
Malawi	80	0·77	335	376	89·1
Nepal	80	0·57	248	259	95·8
Tanzania	100	2·30	999	1042	96·0
India	110	0·19	83	274	30·3
Sri Lanka	110	0·31	135	291	46·4
Guinea	120	0·50	217	314	69·1
Nigeria	120	1·00	435	480	90·6
Madagascar	130	0·52	240	304	78·9
Uganda	130	1·07	478	531	90·2
Kenya	150	0·69	299	447	66·9
Rhodesia	280	0·63	274	838	32·7
Algeria	300	0·02	9	479	1·9
Ivory Coast	310	1·01	438	618	70·9
Zambia	400	0·90	391	900	43·4
Brazil	420	1·60	695	1176	59·1
Cuba	530	0·20	87	1140	7·6
Chile	720	0·31	135	1345	10·4
S. Africa	760	0·04	17	2763	0·6
Venezuela	980	0·63	274	2427	11·3
Greece	1090	0·25	109	1259	8·7
Italy	1760	0·14	61	2492	2·4
Libya	1770	0·20	87	569	15·3
U.S.S.R.	1790	0·36	157	4356	3·6
U.K.	2270	0·01	4	5143	0·1
Finland	2390	1·63	709	4859	14·6
Belgium	2720	0·20	9	5438	0·2
W. Germany	2930	0·03	13	4836	0·3
France	3100	0·12	52	3570	1·5
Canada	3700	0·20	87	8881	1·0
Sweden	4040	0·41	178	5946	3·0
U.S.A.	4760	0·10	43	10 817	0·4

Based on data from: U.N. (1973); I.B.R.D. (1972); F.A.O. (1972).

† For making comparisons between fuels and power on a commercial scale and for measuring the extent of reserves and resources, in this book the unit chosen for convenience is the tonne of coal equivalent, which is equal to 6·9 million kcal or 8000 kilowatt hours.

economic growth which is the harbinger of economic and social change. A shortage of energy will eventually be the most important constraint upon man's material development, but if part of the fuel supply within a country is founded on renewable resources, there will be less danger of economic growth being curtailed by a sudden rise in the price of imported fuel or the depletion of an indigenous resource.

A key to successful development in all countries is the promotion of a viable rural economy. Rural development is an essential part of national development and in order to contribute a surplus of food and raw materials for towns and industry, the countryside must contain an active human resource. If an active rural sector is recognized as an essential ingredient of the development process, the part that the forest fuel resource can play becomes of prime importance. Fuel must be provided for the basic needs of the local population and for many reasons, both social and economic, forest fuel is to be preferred to imported substitutes. If forest land is managed well, surplus fuel could be made available to cities and towns, locally based industries, and possibly for export. The developmental potential of this resource has not been recognized because the market under-prices the fossil fuel resources and ignores or undervalues the benefits obtainable from the renewable forest resource.

2 Energy resources in perspective

The role of energy in the evolution of society

The emergence and development of civilization has been closely associated with an increase in the *per capita* consumption of energy, for example, the use of tools and weapons, control of fire, taming of animals, and cultivation of the soil. Although animal, water, and wind power helped in the evolution of man as a dominant species, there is little doubt that the controlled use of fire was the fact which led to industrialization.

Where forests were available to be 'mined', fuelwood opened up land for colonization in all areas of the world by making available energy for man's survival in new territories. Reynolds and Pierson (1942) state that in the U.S.A. from the earliest settlement until 1900 fuelwood was practically indispensable to a large part of the population. Between 1870 and 1880 when the amount of fuelwood used reached its peak, 1400 million cords of wood were consumed in the decade, equivalent to 134 million tonnes of coal per annum. (This should be compared with the recorded consumption of fuelwood for the whole of Africa for 1972 of 116 million tonnes of coal equivalent (F.A.O. 1974).)

The world's energy

The main sources of the world's energy supply are: solar power, gravitational energy and interior energy. The overall flux and degradation of the earth's supply of energy in watts is shown diagrammatically in Fig. 2.1.

Solar power

The amount of solar power intercepted by the earth can be calculated from the solar constant and the area of the earth's diametrical plane. The solar constant is the quantity of energy which crosses unit area normal to the sun's rays in unit time in free space outside the earth's atmosphere, at a distance from the sun equal to the mean distance to the earth; its value I has been found to be 1·94 calories per minute per square centimetre (Landsberg 1945), which in terms of power is

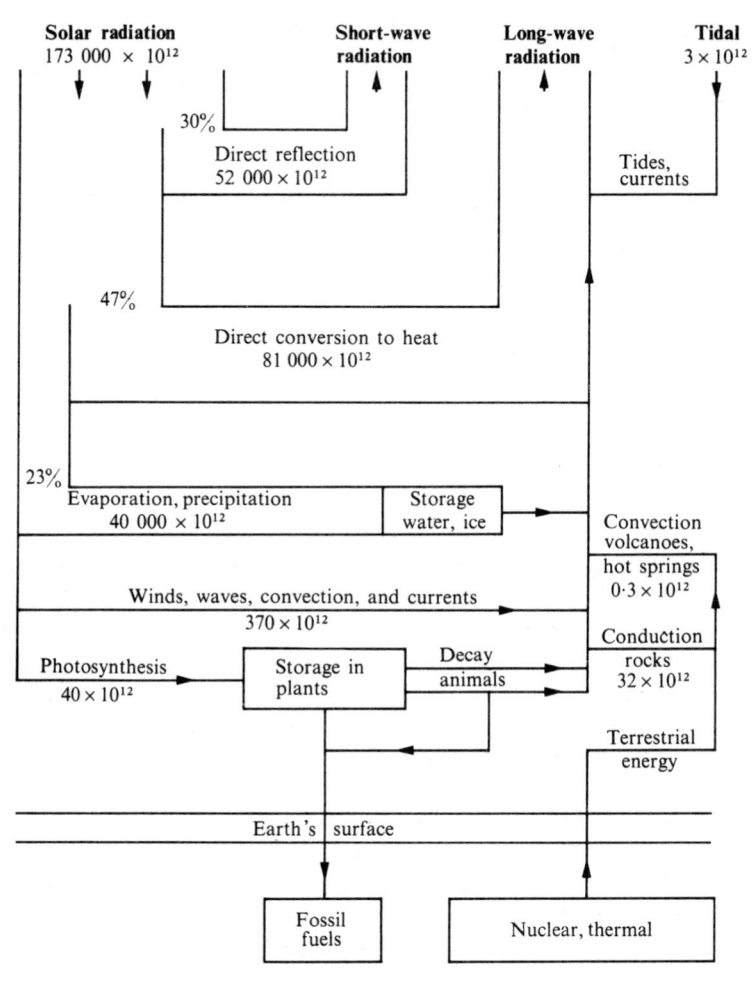

Fig. 2.1. The world's energy flow in watts. Source: Hubbert (1973).

0·135 watts per square centimetre. The solar power intercepted by a sphere is $I\pi r^2$ where I is the solar constant and r is the radius of the sphere. The total solar power P intercepted by the earth is thus $0.135 \times 3.14159 \times (637 \times 10^6)^2 = 173\,000 \times 10^{12}$ W. The flow of energy received by the earth from the sun is more than a thousand times greater than the energy obtained from combined gravitational and interior sources. Of the total solar power, $52\,000 \times 10^{12}$ W is directly reflected back into space as short-wave radiation; $81\,000 \times 10^{12}$ W is converted into heat and absorbed directly by the atmosphere, the oceans, and the lithosphere, a large part of this heat is immediately returned to space as long-wave thermal radiation; 40 000 × 10¹² W of solar energy is responsible for the action of the hydrological cycle; 370 × 10¹² W is taken up by wind, waves, and convection currents; and 40 × 10¹² W of solar energy is used in photosynthesis.

Solar energy captured by photosynthesis and stored in plant and animal tissue is released as thermal energy in phases of the food—energy chain as follows:

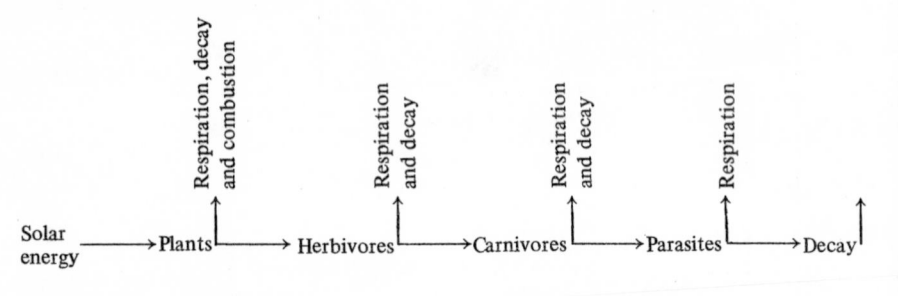

The energy content of any ecosystem is normally constant because the losses of energy from the system are compensated by gains of energy from the photosynthesis process. This dynamic equilibrium state may shift so as to alter the energy flow when animals and plants are introduced or destroyed. Knowledge of this principle enables agriculturists and silviculturists to govern the type and amount of produce obtained by suitably timing the planting and harvesting of crops. Where, however, animal and vegetable material becomes submerged in a reducing environment, a very small fraction of the total photosynthesized energy may be locked up in the fossilized remains as fuel.

A major portion of the world's stored solar energy is contained in deposits of fossil fuel which accumulated over a period of about 500 million years and comprise the coal, gas, and oil resources of the earth. Fossil energy resources are considered to be finite or non-renewable, because additions to the stock are insignificant if judged in relation to the current depletion rate.

Gravitational and interior energy

The sun's planetary system sets in motion the oceanic tides with a potential energy content estimated as 3·0 × 10¹² W.

It is estimated by Roberts (1973) that energy equal to 32 × 10¹² W is escaping from the interior of the earth by thermal conduction, of which only about 0·3 × 10¹² W is lost from volcanoes and hot springs. This energy is thought to be derived mainly from radioactive decay within the earth.

Utilizable energy resources

Apart from the energy obtained from food, most energy used is derived from the sources listed in Table 2.1, in which they are classified according to whether they are finite or renewable.

TABLE 2.1

Classification of energy sources

Energy source	Finite		Renewable
Solar	Fossil coal lignite natural gas oil peat	Photosynthetic	Agricultural bagasse cotton stick dung hay Forest charcoal methanol producer gas wood
		Power	Wind Hydro
Gravitational			Tidal
Interior	Nuclear thorium uranium		Geothermal

Finite energy resources

Fossil. Making estimates of untapped quantities of resources is beset with difficult-ies and lays the evaluator open to attack if subsequent events prove them to be inaccurate. Confusion sometimes arises in the definition of resources and reserves: resources may include stocks of fuel in a condition or situation which makes exploitation under known or expected technological processes extremely unlikely; reserves should satisfy certain criteria for exploitation purposes, especially accessi-bility, and may be divided into measured, indicated, and inferred according to the degree of certainty that they can be exploited. Measured reserves are calculated from geological observations and can almost certainly be considered recoverable under present economic and technical conditions. They may be regarded as known or proven reserves. Indicated reserves are those which might become recoverable from deposits already discovered, account being taken of probable technical and economic development over the next twenty or thirty years. Inferred reserves are those yet unknown and are based almost entirely upon knowledge of the general geological characteristics of the bed or region.

Variations in estimates occur because of the differences in the specifications used in the investigations. These specifications depend upon the envisaged future intensity of extraction, itself determined by unknown economic forces and tech-nological advance. Estimates also tend to reflect the views of the individual or organization making the forecast, which may be pessimistic or optimistic. For this reason the motivation for the estimate is often worth investigating when examining the available data.

Fig. 2.2 sets out diagrammatically the main factors affecting the rate of recovery of fuel resources, based on the assumption that there is an absolute limit to the amount available.

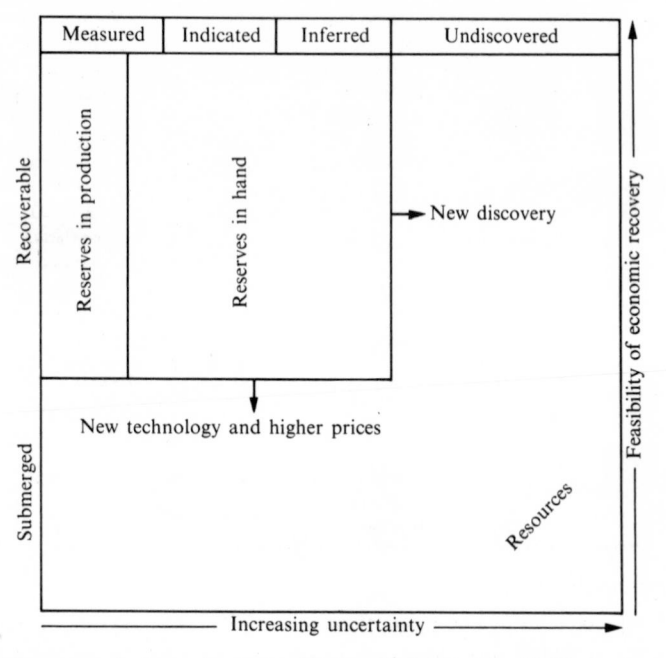

Fig. 2.2. The economic, imponderable, and technological factors affecting estimates of fossil fuel reserves and resources.

Reserves of fossil fuels although large are concentrated in relatively few areas. Consequently, the two most important factors which are likely to affect economic development, because of the unevenness of the distribution of reserves throughout the world, are the rise in prices which will accompany the increasing demand for fuel from diminishing resources, and the restrictions imposed by exporting countries upon the supply to all areas of demand.

The total initial reserves of fossil fuels are estimated to have amounted to 3 227 000 million tonnes CE. The relative importance in terms of the initial amount and the proportion of each type of fuel consumed prior to 1970 are shown in Table 2.2. Of all the fossil fuel reserves remaining, about three-quarters is represented by coal. At the annual rate of increase in energy consumption 1967–70, all mineable coal reserves will be exhausted by A.D. 2100. Oil reserves, which on present estimates are expected to last 17 years, will be extended until 2002 if indicated and inferred reserves and oil from tar sands and oil shales are included. Natural gas reserves are expected to last until 2012.

TABLE 2.2

Total estimated initial recoverable reserves of fossil fuels and amount consumed and remaining, 1970

Fuel	Initial reserve (tonnes CE x 10^9)	Consumed to 1970 (tonnes CE x 10^9)	Remaining in 1970 (tonnes CE x 10^9)	Percentage of initial reserve consumed
Coal	2477[1]	177	2300	7·1
Oil	285[2]	44	241	15·4
Natural Gas	362[3]	19	343	5·2
Oil (shale)	40[3]	–	40	0·0
Oil (tar sands)	63[3]	–	63	0·0
TOTAL	3227	240	2987	Av. 7·6

Source: (1) Averitt (1961); (2) Warman (1971); (3) Hubbert (1973).

Nuclear. Nuclear energy may be obtained from two contrasting processes: fission and fusion. In each case the mass of the reaction products is slightly less than that of the reactants and the lost mass is converted into energy in accordance with the equation relating mass to energy.

The development of large-scale power supplies by fissioning uranium 235 depends upon finding solutions to three fundamental problems: maintenance of the low-cost supply of uranium; safe disposal of the extremely dangerous fission products; and development of fail-safe production processes.

Energy is produced from fusion when atoms of isotopes of light elements in the atomic scale are fused to form heavier elements, e.g. deuterium (an isotope of hydrogen) may be converted to helium. The huge potential energy outputs available from relatively abundant isotopes and the fact that the end-products are not radioactive make the achievement of controlled fusion one of the most important goals of nuclear science.

Table 2.3 shows the estimated reserves of finite energy in 1970. The amounts consumed in that year have been extrapolated at the exponential growth rate obtained over the four years 1967–70 in order to produce an eco-doomster's estimate of the probable life of the reserves. Obviously price will influence demand to a great extent and the consumption rate will decrease as the reserves become depleted but the table is useful in that it indicates that oil and natural gas are likely to become very much dearer because of the smaller reserves and this will undoubtedly also increase the price of coal.

TABLE 2.3

The world's finite energy reserves, in tonnes $\times 10^9$ CE, projected to A.D. 2000 and to depletion date at 1970 consumption and growth rates

	Coal	Oil[1]	Natural gas	Uranium[2] Breeder	Light-water
Reserves 1970	2300	344	343	7900	113
Growth rates 1967–70	2½%	7½%	7½%	15%	
Accumulated consumption to A.D. 2000 if present growth maintained	106	295	147	280[2]	4
Reserves A.D. 2000	2194	49	196	7620	109
Years to depletion from 1970[3]	130	32	42	84	52

[1] Includes oil contained in shale and tar sands

[2] Energy reserves are increased by a factor of 70 if breeder reactors are used. It has been assumed that natural uranium is the main fuel until 2000

† [3] The calculation of number of years to depletion was made by the use of the formula $Vn = \left\{ r(1+i)^n - 1 \right\} / i$, where

Vn = reserve; r = consumption (1970); i = growth rate (coal 0·025, oil, and gas 0·075; n = number of years to depletion.

Renewable energy resources

Photosynthetic. Cow dung is widely used as a domestic cooking fuel in Bangladesh, India, Nepal, Pakistan, Turkey and other countries in the Middle East (see Table 2.4). It is reasonable to assume that the present annual consumption of cow dung is not less than 150 million tonnes (90 million tonnes CE), and fairly safe to assume that the total consumption of agricultural wastes, e.g. bagasse, cotton sticks, and hay, as fuel is not more than 10 million tonnes of coal equivalent.

TABLE 2.4

Estimated annual consumption of cow dung as fuel

Country	Million tonnes	Million tonnes CE
India[1]	100	58·0
Pakistan[2]	11	6·3
Turkey[3]	14	8·1

Sources: [1] National Commission on Agriculture (India) (1972)
[2] Lerche and Khan (1970)
[3] T.T.K.C. (1962)

Forests provide the fuel for most of the world's population but because wood is consumed mostly in the domestic economies of the developing countries, it appears as a comparatively modest part of the world's total fuel consumption. Consumption of fuelwood in 1970 amounted to 487 million tonnes of coal equivalent and is increasing at the rate of approximately 1 per cent per annum, see Table 2.5.

TABLE 2.5

World fuelwood removals 1967–70 (including wood for charcoal)

Year	million m^3	million tonnes CE
1967	1096	477
1968	1108	482
1969	1115	485
1970	1120	487

Source: F.A.O. (1974)

There are signs that an increasing amount of wood is being converted to charcoal in developing countries as urbanization sets in, mainly because of transport advantage, convenience, and the desire for cleaner air. Earl (1973a) estimates that the total recorded production of charcoal in 1970 was about 3 million tonnes (approximately 3·1 million tonnes CE) but the exact figure, which is much higher, is unknown because of the lack of adequate statistics from many countries. Wood is also the primary raw material for liquid and gas fuels e.g. methyl alcohol, producer gas, water gas, etc.

Power. Of the renewable power sources only hydro-electricity presents a serious challenge to the dominant role at present taken by finite power generation. This is not to imply that other sources are not important but in the global scene their contribution is essentially marginal. If the water power of the world were fully developed and the plants worked at about 50 per cent of capacity, electricity production would amount to 12×10^{12} kW h or 1500 million tonnes CE. If this electrical energy were to be produced by fossil fuel the amount needed (assuming a 30 per cent efficiency) would be approximately 5000 million tonnes of coal.

TABLE 2.6

The world's renewable energy resources[†] and projected consumption in A.D. 2000 if present growth rates continue

	Hydro	Geother-mal	Tidal	Solar	Wood and Charcoal	Dung	Agricul-tural waste
			(million tonnes CE)				
Maximum possible energy production from resources available in 1970	1500	33	35	–	7584	90	10
Growth rate 1967–70	5½%	–	–	–	1%	–	–
Estimated consumption in year 2000 at present growth rates for hydro-electric and wood and assuming full utilization of geo-thermal and tidal sources	750	33	35	–	656	90	10

† Excludes wind and animal power

TABLE 2.7
The world's recorded energy consumption 1967–70 in million tonnes CE

Year	Finite				Renewable							Total
	Coal	Oil	Natural gas	Uranium	Hydroelectric	Geothermal	Tidal†	Solar†	Wood and Charcoal	Dung	Agricultural waste	
1967	2175	2218	1092	5	127	1	–	–	477	90	10	6195
1968	2281	2415	1189	7	131	1	–	–	482	90	10	6606
1969	2357	2608	1303	8	140	1	–	–	485	90	10	7002
1970	2419	2850	1418	10	150	1	–	–	487	90	10	7435
Average annual growth 1967–70	2½%	7½%	7½%	15%	5½%	–	–	–	1%	–	–	6%–7%

Sources: U.N. (1973); F.A.O. (1974); Others   † Not significant at present.

Table 2.6 places the potential of renewable energy resources in perspective. It can be seen that the estimated annual energy increment from the designated forest areas of the world is five times the capacity of the world's hydro-electric potential, if fully developed, and more than the world's total annual consumption of fossil fuel in 1970. If the consumption of wood for both timber and fuel purposes is excluded from the total estimated annual increment of wood, the unused portion amounts to 6700 million tonnes of coal equivalent.

Table 2.7 gives the total recorded consumption of energy from all sources from 1967–70 in coal equivalents. It can be seen that more than 90 per cent of the world's consumption of energy is derived from the non-renewable fuels, especially coal, oil, and natural gas.

The important questions which affect the future of economic activity are: how much longer can fossil fuels continue to be exploited before substitution of alternative fuels become economic; and if, as it seems likely, there is going to be a serious shortfall, what preparations, if any, can be made to meet it?

Preparations for obtaining a greater share of total energy consumption from alternative sources should not be confined to nuclear fission and fusion but should extend to other energy sources, especially forests, which are not only renewable but also relatively pollution-free.

3 The energy value of forest fuel

'More than 50 per cent of the world's annual wood production
is utilized as fuel and of this, 90 per cent is used in
the developing world.'
F.A.O. (1971)

The comparative value of fuels

An understanding of the technical potential and versatility of wood as a source of
fuel is a prerequisite to meaningful economic analysis of projects involving the
conversion or establishment of forests for the production of energy.

The majority of fuels (other than nuclear fuels) depend for their thermal effect
on the combustion of the carbon and hydrogen which they contain. In the absence
of moisture, coal, charcoal, oil, and natural gas consist almost entirely of carbon
and hydrogen (85–7 per cent carbon, 11–13 per cent hydrogen). The presence
of oxygen in lignite, peat, and wood has the effect of lessening their value as fuels.

When fuels are compared, the figure usually quoted for the calorific value is
the gross value, which includes the heat derived from the condensation of any
water vapour produced by combustion to liquid water. The water vapour may be
derived either from free moisture present in the fuel, or from the combustion of
hydrogen present in the fuel in chemical combination. The net calorific value
does not include the heat obtained from the condensation of water vapour, and
is lower than the gross calorific value by this amount. Unless otherwise stated,
the values quoted hereafter will be gross.

TABLE 3.1
Approximate calorific value of some common fuels

Fuel	Calorific value
Paraffin	10·4
Fuel oil	9·8
Charcoal	7·1
Coal (bituminous)	6·9
Wood, oven-dry (0% m.c.)	4·7
Dung, air-dry	4·0
Peat, air-dry	4·0
Wood, air-dry (25–30% m.c.)	3·5

Forest energy is most commonly obtained from fuelwood and charcoal, to a
lesser extent from the liquid and gaseous products of wood distillation, or from

producer and water gas, obtained from wood and charcoal. Although derived from the same organic forest source, the various fuels differ in both calorific value and physical properties, giving great flexibility of choice to the consumer. For example, in conditions of forest abundance wood is often the most practical solid fuel for heating and cooking purposes; charcoal would be the most suitable choice for meeting a requirement for smokeless fuel, whilst for certain types of engine requiring a very high-octane fuel, methanol may be ideal. Producer gas may be the most practical fuel for many industrial uses.

Primary forest fuel

Wood is composed principally of cellulose and ligno-cellulose together with gums, resins, inorganic matter, and a variable amount of moisture, the amount depending on the kind of wood, the season in which it is cut, and the extent to which it has been allowed to dry. The approximate proportions by weight of the main elements present in wood are: carbon 50 per cent, hydrogen 6 per cent, oxygen 44 per cent, and a trace of nitrogen.

    The simplest and easiest way of obtaining forest energy is from the combustion of wood. Fuelwood can be obtained from any tree whether occurring naturally or planted, either directly from the forest or from waste material produced at saw-mills and wood-using industries. It is very simple to prepare and use and is the raw material for the more sophisticated secondary forest energy sources such as charcoal, methyl alcohol (CH_3OH), producer gas (CO), water gas ($CO + H_2$), hydrogen (H_2), and electricity.

    The gross calorific value of oven-dry wood averages 4·7. Conifers usually have a slightly above-average value of approximately 4·8 and may exceed 5·0. The low specific gravity of wood does not affect the calorific value (which is based on unit weight), but it does, of course, affect the heat value per unit volume which usually makes the light, solid fuels less desirable than the heavy. Table 3.2 gives a range of values of specific gravity from some selected trees which may be compared with some values of common fuels in Table 3.3. The ash content of wood is usually low, from 0·5–5 per cent and is of little consequence.

    The most important controllable factor influencing the efficiency of wood as a fuel is the moisture content. Moisture in very fresh wood may amount to more than 100 per cent of the dry weight substance which reduces its value as fuel because of the absorption of heat required in the evaporation of water. It is customary in the timber trade to estimate moisture as a percentage of the dry material. This convention is used for both fuelwood and charcoal. For example, wood is said to have a moisture content of 100 per cent if 2 kilograms of fresh wood after drying at 104°C to constant weight are found to weigh 1 kilogram. If in the above example the moisture had been determined on a 'wet weight' basis the wood would have appeared to have contained only 50 per cent and not 100 per cent moisture and thus the calorific value would have been incorrectly calculated as 3·3 kcal/g when in fact it was only 2·5. The difference between the calorific values calculated on a 'dry weight' basis and on a 'wet weight' basis are shown in Table 3.4.

TABLE 3.2

Specific gravity of woods from a few selected trees

Species	s.g. (air-dry)	Country	Remarks
Alnus rubra	0·46	U.S.A.	Yields of 43 tonnes/ha/year in Canada. Possible use in energy plantations.
Eucalyptus saligna	0·70	E. Africa S. America	Yields of 40−50 tonnes/ha/year Widespread plantations
Picea sitchensis	0·46	U.K.	Yields of 12 tonnes/ha/year Widespread plantations
Maesopsis eminii	0·54	Uganda	Yields of 15 tonnes/ha/year Widely planted

TABLE 3.3

Specific gravity of some common fuels

Fuel	s.g.
Coal (bituminous)	1·1
Oil (fuel)	0·9
Paraffin	0·8
Charcoal	0·4

TABLE 3.4

Comparison between the percentage moisture content and calorific value of wood, determined on a dry weight and wet weight basis

Percentage moisture		Calorific value (kcal/g)	
Dry	Wet	Dry	Wet
0·0	0·0	5·0	5·0
10·0	9·1	4·5	4·5
25·0	20·0	4·0	4·2
50·0	33·3	3·3	4·0
100·0	50·0	2·5	3·3
200·0	66·7	1·7	3·0

The reduction of the moisture content in wood to be used as fuel is desirable for two main reasons: to reduce handling and transport costs; and to increase its fuel value. Wood for use as a primary fuel is usually cut 3−4 months before use in the tropics and 6−12 months in temperate zones in order that the moisture content should be reduced to 25−30 per cent, resulting in an increase in the calorific value to between 3·5 and 4·0 (Earl 1973a). For most purposes fuelwood is prepared and stacked in cords, cubic yards, or stères (stacked m³) to facilitate easy checking and assessment of payment due to the men, but as a factor input in industry it is usually accounted for on a weight basis. There can be considerable discrepancy between the expected and actual weight of wood obtained from stacks because of the free moisture. The effect of differences in length and diameter and the incidence of knots and crookedness also plays a major part in determining the amount of solid wood contained in stacks. Stacks consisting of short lengths of large diameter wood contain more solid volume than stacks with small diameter wood in long lengths, and stacks containing straight, short pieces have more volume content than stacks with long, crooked, or knotty pieces. Troup (1926) produced a table of reducing factors for stacked fuel which makes allowance for most of these effects, see Table 3.5

TABLE 3.5

Reducing factors for converting stacked wood to solid wood content

Species	Diameter class of material	Reducing factor
Conifer	Large round and straight	0·80
	Medium split billets smooth and straight	0·75
	Medium split billets crooked	0·70
	Small round firewood	0·70
Hardwood	Large split billets smooth and straight	0·70
	Large split billets crooked	0·65
	Small round firewood smooth and straight	0·65
	Small round firewood crooked	0·55
Small branches and twigs	Small round firewood crooked	0·30–0·45
Brushwood	Small round firewood crooked	0·15–0·20

The solid volume content of a stère of wood ranges from 0·80–0·45 m³ and thus a stack of the latter will contain only 56 per cent of the energy of a stack of the former. The relationship between stacked and solid volume content of various categories of fuelwood should be established and drying curves prepared before large-scale operations are undertaken.

The advantages and disadvantages of wood fuel are as follows.

ADVANTAGES

In many developing countries it is the cheapest fuel available, not only per tonne but also per unit of heat.

When properly dried it burns safely and easily so that semi-skilled labour may soon be taught to use it with economy. Skilled labour is, however, required for use with the highly efficient, latest types of furnaces.

DISADVANTAGES

Labour intensive which makes it expensive in regions where wages are high.

Without properly organized management the forests become quickly depleted. Its use requires organization and co-operation with forest departments and other land users.

Regular supplies may be uneven in quality (this can be minimized with good control).

ADVANTAGES	DISADVANTAGES
No special storage facilities are required apart from open space.	The calorific value is lower than that of fossil fuels.
It is perfectly safe to store for long periods.	A large stacking space is required near the place of use.

Apart from general domestic purposes wood is used to provide heat in many industries, e.g. brickworks, distilleries, hand-made paper works, jaggeries, potteries, sugar works, tea factories, tile-works, and tobacco barns. It also provides steam for mechanical energy in sawmills, steam locomotives, and boats, and may be used to generate electricity for use in small industries or on a large scale.

Secondary forest fuel

Secondary forest fuels are produced as a result of the conversion of primary woody material to more valuable fuels by carbonization, distillation, or gasification.

Carbonization

The simplest method of up-grading the value of wood as a fuel is to convert it to charcoal. A detailed study of charcoal was made by the writer during the tenure of an F.A.O. Andre Mayer Research Fellowship (Earl 1973a). Charcoal is produced as a result of the chemical reduction of organic material under controlled conditions. It is commonly used as a secondary energy source and as a chemical agent in industry but also has many other important uses. For those countries with sufficient manpower and forest resources charcoal has special significance for development.

The carbonization process can be separated into four stages.

STAGE	APPROXIMATE TEMPERATURE	PRODUCTS
1. Combustion (kilns only)	Ambient to 600°C, then down to stage 2 temperature	Carbon dioxide Water
2. Dehydration	$100-120^{\circ}$C	Water
3. Exothermic	Starts at 270°C; rises to $400-600^{\circ}$C	Acetic acid Alcohol Carbon dioxide Carbon monoxide Hydrogen Methane Methyl alcohol Nitrogen Pitch Tar Water
4. Cooling	$400-600^{\circ}$C to ambient	Nil

Approximately 4·7 million kcal are contained in a tonne of oven dry wood
and 7·1 million in a tonne of charcoal. There is a loss of about 2·6 million kcal
(55 per cent) per tonne of wood converted to charcoal, assuming a 30 per cent
yield of charcoal, but in practical terms this loss is below 30 per cent because
air-dried fuelwood contains not more than 3·5 million kcal per tonne. No special
energy is required for carbonization in kilns since all the necessary energy is
provided from the combustion of part of the wood charge; and if the by-products
from wood distillation are collected, energy inputs roughly equivalent to the
amounts lost during carbonization without recovery of by-products are needed.
Thus although conversion results in a decrease in the total available energy yield,
its advantage may lie in the more desirable properties of the products obtained
(see p. 33).

The nature and properties of wood charcoal. The physical and chemical properties of charcoal depend partly upon those of the original material from which it
is made and partly upon the conditions of the carbonization process. Most, but
not all, fuel users prefer charcoal which does not break easily, can be ignited
readily, and will continue to emit heat for a long time. Charcoal of acceptable
quality is sometimes obtained by traders who mix different charcoals together
to get a 'proprietary blend'. Such blending often took place in Uganda, where
soft, quick-burning Eucalyptus charcoal was mixed with hard *Acacia* charcoal.
In the United Kingdom one charcoal manufacturer sells his product in two packs,
one pack containing quick-igniting charcoal made from *Pinus* and the second
containing slow-burning hardwood charcoal. This enterprising company markets
the *Pinus* charcoal at a premium and recommends it for starting barbecues.

The following summarizes the general features of wood charcoal.

Yield by weight	20–30% of the dry weight of wood
Yield by volume	50% of the volume of wood
Percentage yield of lump charcoal i.e.	
> 2·5 cm	75–90%
Specific gravity	
(a) apparent	0·2–0·5
(b) real	1·3–1·5
Specific surface area	
(a) lump charcoal	1–2 m^2/g
(b) activated charcoal	300–2000 m^2/g
Stability	Inert when conditioned 24 hours
Hardness	Varies with density of wood used
Moisture	1–16%
Volatile matter (mainly hydrocarbon)	7–30%
Fixed carbon	80–90%
Calorific value	Approximately 7·1
Sulphur	Trace
Phosphorus	Trace
Ash	0·5–10%

Charcoal for industrial use and for activation usually has to meet precise
specifications. These can be fulfilled only if the end-product has been made from

suitable species, necessary adjustments of the carbonization process have been carried out, and appropriate methods of analysis have been used to ensure quality control during production.

The raw materials for charcoal. Most charcoal is made from wood although there are other less abundant materials, e.g. coconut shell and bone, which provide very important and valuable charcoals for specialized use. The two most important raw material sources are roundwood and wood residues, the former being the most abundant. Roundwood can be produced in fuel plantations or as a subsidiary operation to other forestry or land-clearing schemes. The stems and branches from softwoods and hardwoods and the stems of palm trees can usually be converted to lump charcoal which can be used as fuel without further treatment. Wood residues often contain a high proportion of bark but apart from giving rise to a slightly more dusty and friable product the quality is suitable for general fuel purposes. The high inorganic content of carbonized bark compared with that of wood charcoal rules out its use for specialized purposes, e.g. in cement manufacture, but it provides a readily-saleable product in Japan and in the U.S.A. after it is crushed and briquetted.

Dry wood usually produces greater yields of charcoal than wet wood and the time needed for carbonization is shorter. Moisture can be removed by air-seasoning wood before carbonization and thus it is usually advisable to cut and split material to the desired size when green, to provide the greatest surface area possible for evaporation. It is not, however, imperative to use dry wood, for reasonably good results have been achieved with wood containing 100 per cent moisture or more. The moisture content of the initial wood charge does not appear to affect the quality of the charcoal produced (Earl 1973a), and in practice it may be preferable to sacrifice some charcoal yield for the advantage of a quicker return on the money expended on wood preparation.

One practical point which should not be over-looked is that dried wood is lighter than wet wood. This is an important consideration for the people doing the work. For example, 6 stères of wood at 100 per cent moisture content, prepared for a portable steel kiln in the tropics, would weigh approximately 4 tonnes; but after 3 months and with the moisture down to 40 per cent there would be a tonne less to handle. If this is multiplied by 12 (the number of firings in a month) the men loading wet wood would have lifted 12 tonnes more water than men loading the dried wood. This would have been equivalent to loading another 4 kilns, if the energy expended had been used instead on lifting wood at 40 per cent moisture content.

Carbonization techniques. Although techniques differ widely, the basic principle is common to all of them and the types of appliances may be divided into kilns, retorts, continuous kilns, and furnaces.

In kilning, part of the charge provides the energy needed to initiate carbonization. Kilns have evolved from the earliest means of making charcoal known to man, i.e. by covering burning wood with turf or by firing the wood in a hole in the ground (Plate 1). The principle involved in all kilns is similar and depends upon the combustion of part of a pile of wood until it is hot enough to be able to react exothermically in a limited air supply, i.e. to carbonize.

The method of manufacturing charcoal in earth or pit kilns has the advantages that wood handling is reduced to a minimum, and little or no capital expenditure is required for equipment. The disadvantages are that yields are uncertain and often low, the charcoal is variable in quality and is sometimes mixed with soil and stones, and carbonization time is lengthy and difficult to control. These variables make it extremely difficult to forecast yields and profits and the situation is further complicated by the fact that the persons concerned seldom keep any records.

From the simple earth-covered kilns and pits have evolved those built of brick, concrete, and metal, which have the advantage of giving better control and a cleaner end-product (Plates 2 and 3). For forest refining operations portable steel kilns have been developed which have advantages over fixed installations in many situations. A description of a low-cost kiln developed in Uganda and now working successfully in at least eight countries is given by Earl (1973a).

Retorts are containers in which wood is subjected to heat applied to the external surface of the apparatus until the charge is converted to charcoal. The gases produced, if collected and condensed, may be fractionated into saleable products such as methyl alcohol, acetic acid, and pitch. The process is termed 'wood distillation' when these by-products are collected (see p. 33). Any advantage of retorting over kilning depends upon the existence of a market for the by-products because of the high capital costs involved (Plate 4).

Continuous kilns have been developed in the U.S.A. for the continuous production of charcoal and are erroneously referred to as retorts. The apparatus usually consists of a vertical insulated steel cylinder in which raw material enters at the top and charcoal is withdrawn from the bottom. In a continuous kiln, energy from an external fuel source is usually passed into the charge for at least part of the carbonization cycle. No by-product recovery is attempted. The use of continuous kilns is likely to be restricted to specialized situations where labour is available by day and night in order that a constant supply of small wood can be fed into the kiln as required by the process.

The Herreschoff furnace has been a most important development in the field of wood carbonization. Wood chips are carried continuously through the furnace under controlled conditions. Although an external energy source is needed to initiate the process and for driving the charge through, the energy derived from the exothermic reaction of part of the charge provides all the heat needed for continuous carbonization.

Advantages and disadvantages of the various carbonization systems

ADVANTAGES	DISADVANTAGES
Kilns	
Low capital costs.	Labour-intensive (developed countries).
No external fuel requirement.	Quality and quantity of charcoal difficult to control.
Low-technological requirement.	
Labour-intensive (developing countries).	By-products (energy) lost.
Aid to silviculture—portable kilns provide very good regeneration sites.	Very small material, e.g. chips, sawdust, and bark cannot easily be utilized.
Relatively large pieces of wood may be used. Moisture content not critical.	
Retorts	
Not labour-intensive (developed countries).	Capital-intensive (developing countries).
High yield of charcoal with built-in quality control.	Advanced technology needed.
By-products may be more valuable than required energy inputs.	Size and moisture content of wood has to be strictly controlled.
	External energy source required for at least part of the process.
Continuous kilns	
Can utilize small-sized residues.	Charcoal is hot when discharged and therefore requires special handling.
Provide continuous supplies of good quality charcoal.	Attention needed day and night.
Cheaper than retorts and furnaces.	By-products lost.
	Require external energy inputs for at least part of the time.
Furnaces	
Can utilize any organic material including wood chips, sawdust, and bark.	Capital intensive.
Provide continuous supplies of high quality charcoal of any desired volatile content.	Wood has to be chipped.
	Moisture content must be below 45%.
Not labour-intensive (developed countries).	Advanced technology required.
	By-products lost.

The main outlets for charcoal.

Charcoal as a fuel for domestic purposes. As charcoal is smokeless and almost sulphur-free, it is an ideal fuel for towns and cities and can be used in stoves capable of heating the home and providing hot water as well as being adapted for general cooking. The price is often high in developed countries but in countries where wood is plentiful it may be the cheapest smokeless fuel available. It is especially suitable for grilling and barbecuing because it imparts a delicious and distinctive flavour to the food.

Charcoal as a fuel for industrial purposes. Charcoal can be used for direct drying purposes, for example, for maturing and curing hops, tobacco and other commodities where a special atmosphere is required. In the United Kingdom nearly all the hop drying was done with charcoal before the shortage of supplies led to an increase in its price and its replacement by cheaper fuels (which are, however, not as good for the purpose).

Charcoal can also be used for indirect drying purposes, for example, in central heating systems in which hot air or water are circulated. It is used in such systems for heating tobacco barns; for this purpose it has no special advantage over other fuels but where fuelwood supplies are obtainable only at some distance from the centre of consumption it might be more economic to carbonize the fuelwood in order to reduce transport costs (see Fig. 6.1).

Charcoal can be used as an internal fuel in lime and cement manufacture. It is mixed with limestone and fired to obtain quicklime or pulverized and used in place of oil in fuel-injection equipment; its main application as pulverized fuel has been in the manufacture of cement—approximately 1 tonne of charcoal is needed to make 4 tonnes of Portland cement.

In metal extraction, the strong reducing properties of charcoal are used. Although it is acknowledged to be as good as, if not better than, coke, there are practical difficulties in obtaining adequate supplies to feed the large iron and steel works which are needed to achieve economies of scale. The charcoal-iron industries working successfully in Brazil, Argentina, Malaysia, Australia, and India have large forests available for the production of charcoal. Its use for iron-smelting is likely to be most profitable where it can contribute to lessen the silvicultural costs of increasing the productivity of the forest.

Other uses of charcoal occur in water purification and sewage works. It can also be used in the production of artists' materials, cyanide, carbide, and carbon disulphide, fireworks and gunpowder, pigments for printing and paints, plastics, poultry and animal feeds, and rubber.

TABLE 3.6
The main technical advantages and disadvantages of charcoal

Advantages	Disadvantages
Almost smokeless when burnt and produces a fire-bed from which a high proportion of the energy is emitted as radiant heat.	Its low bulk density necessitates special transporting and storage arrangements.
It is readily ground to a fine powder and then may be used with standard equipment in pulverized fuel firing.	It is rather fragile and is easily broken during handling or by compression. This does not affect the calorific value but can be a disadvantage if lump fuel is particularly required.
The calorific value is similar to that of high-quality coal.	
It acts as a strong reducing agent when heated.	As with all fuels with a high carbon content, care has to be taken during combustion to ensure that there is free circulation of air because of the danger of carbon monoxide poisoning.
It has many industrial uses.	

Increasing the value of charcoal. Lump charcoal can be powdered and mixed with charcoal fines, together with wood tar or starch, to form briquettes. Usually the mixture is pressed into moulds and oven-dried, although heat is not strictly necessary. The main advantages of briquetting are:

(1) Low wastage: the total yield of charcoal including dust can be utilized.
(2) Cheaper transport and storage: briquettes, with no additive other than a binder, are denser than lump charcoal and therefore have more thermal content per unit volume. Briquettes can also be made to a standard size thus facilitating easy packing. They are particularly useful for producer-gas units in vehicles because of the smaller storage space required as compared with lump charcoal.
(3) Burning quality: the burning quality of briquettes can be modified by the addition of substances chosen so as to suit the consumer, e.g. wood chips to improve the flavour of barbecued meat, or chemicals to produce rapidly ignitable but slow-burning properties.

Briquetting increases the value and price of charcoal but it is a capital-intensive process and is therefore recommended only where there is a good domestic market for barbecue fuel and where waste wood is available cheaply near a port from which an export market can be generated. It may be particularly valuable in dealing with transport problems in developing countries by providing a very good fuel for producer-gas units. For this reason it has very great developmental prospects. A small hand-operated briquetting machine might be usefully developed in order to utilize waste charcoal fines; this warrants further research as an intermediate technology project.

Activated charcoal, with a very large internal surface area ranging from 300–2000 square metres per gram, is much more reactive than ordinary charcoal with a specific surface area of only one or two square metres per gram. Because of this vast surface area, activated charcoal is highly absorptive of gases and liquids, and this makes it one of the most valuable forest products.

During pyrolysis or carbonization of organic materials, most of the oxygen and hydrogen are removed. The remaining carbon is in the form of irregular masses with the interstices partly filled by disorganized amorphous carbon arising from the decomposition of the wood tars. This blocking of the interstices gives the carbonized product a comparatively low capacity for absorption.

Charcoal can be partially activated by heating it in a stream of inert gas or by using a suitable solvent or chemical to dissolve or react with the tarry products. To attain the maximum possible power of absorption, the charcoal has to be activated under conditions whereby the agent used reacts with the carbon.

There are two main manufacturing processes for activated charcoal.

(1) Zinc chloride, or some other activating chemical, is mixed with the wood and carbonized to 500–900°C in a retort. The charcoal is cooled and washed to remove and recover the activating chemical, then filtered and dried. Usually the charcoal is finely divided; if not, it is ground to a powder before use.

(2) The raw material is first carbonized at 400–500°C and then activated in granular form to develop the porosity and surface area by means of steam, carbon dioxide, or chlorine at a temperature of 800–1000°C.

There are two commercial types of activated charcoal, distinguished, according to their usual application for use with gases or liquids, by the terms gas-phase and liquid-phase. Gas-phase carbons are hard, dense granules or pellets which are used principally for absorbing gases and vapours; liquid phase carbons are light, fluffy powders which are used principally for decolourizing liquids.

World-wide interest has been aroused in activated charcoal because of its potential for preventing and combating the results of pollution. Some of the more notable recent discoveries have been as follows: herbicidal deactivation in the soil; insecticidal deactivation in mammals; sewage treatment; air purification; and water purification.

The activation process has very great developmental possibilities for countries with suitable raw materials, particularly coniferous residues and coconut shells, and good export outlets because of the enormous value-added potential of this type of charcoal.

Distillation

Wood distillation has been studied extensively for centuries and is known to have been practised by the Egyptians, who recovered tar and pyroligneous acid from wood for use in their embalming processes. Retorts were developed in Europe and the U.S.A. for the commercial production of acetic acid, methanol, and acetone until these products were synthesized more cheaply from petrochemicals; this led to the decline of the wood-distillation industry in the first quarter of the present century.

In distillation, the wood charge is heated in a closed container so arranged that all gases and liquids evolved pass out through a condenser. The non-condensable gases can be utilized as an energy source and the condensed gas and water-soluble tar collected, from whence they can be decanted and fractionally distilled to give useful organic chemical products.

Harbottle, in an unpublished report written in 1969, gave an average breakdown of the products obtainable from tropical woods in a Lambiotte retort, based on some limited laboratory-scale runs on *Maesopsis eminii*, *Eucalyptus robusta* and a mixed forest batch (Table 3.7).

In the same 1969 report Harbottle gave the following uses for by-products: gas for burning as fuel; methyl alcohol as an industrial solvent and for possible preparation of methyl esters of fatty acids with glycerine by-product, and for fuel for internal combustion and jet engines; acetic acid for conversion to acetone and also for use in the textile industry; acetone as an industrial solvent; wood oil, some fractions are in world demand, end use unspecified; creosote for timber preservation; and pitch for road-making when blended with asphalt.

TABLE 3.7
Average products available from tropical woods

Yields per 1000 kilograms of dry wood	
Charcoal	300 kg
Gas (calorific value approximately 2500 kcal/m^3)	140 m^3
Methyl alcohol	14 litres
Acetic acid	53 litres
Esters (mainly methyl acetate and ethyl formate)	8 litres
Acetone	3 litres
Wood oil and light tar	76 litres
Creosote oil	12 litres
Pitch	30 kg

In Australia, methyl alcohol is used as an aviation spirit and acetic acid is used in the pickling industry. Methyl alcohol is a very high octane fuel with anti-knock properties and could reasonably be blended with petroleum in order to achieve substantial economies in consumption of fuels used for road transport. At present most methyl alcohol is used to denature ethyl alcohol—a relatively unimportant role

Yashenko (1971) reports that some useful work on pitch has been done in the U.S.S.R. Wood tar obtained from carbonized wood waste was mixed with 1·5—3·0 per cent limestone which increased the viscosity and cohesion of the tar and improved the water and low temperature resistance of tar reinforced foundations in highway construction. The mechanical strength and malleability of the foundations can be brought up to desired standards by varying the limestone content in the tar.

That these distillates are not widely utilized at the present time is because large quantities of fossil fuels exist, which can be won and distilled at less cost than that involved in growing, cutting, and treating wood. It is perhaps reasonable to suggest that over the next 30 years if coal and oil become more expensive relative to wood, the products of wood distillation may once again in certain situations become competitive with chemicals produced from oil and coal.

Gasification. The two gases commonly obtained from controlled heating of wood and charcoal are producer gas and water gas.

Producer gas consists of carbon monoxide and nitrogen produced by burning carbon in a supply of air insufficient to convert it into carbon dioxide. The reaction is strongly exothermic:

$$2C + O_2 = 2CO + (2 \times 26 \cdot 8) \, kcal$$

If the gas is to be used in furnaces it is burned immediately after production, so that its heat of formation is not wasted. If, however, it is required for internal combustion engines it must be washed before use, and there is then considerable loss of heat.

Water gas is a mixture of carbon monoxide and hydrogen (with small quantities of carbon dioxide and nitrogen), made by driving steam or a fine spray of water over incandescent charcoal. This reaction is endothermic:

$$C + H_2O = CO + H_2 - 28{\cdot}0 \text{ kcal}$$

The water gas so obtained is either burned or used as a source of hydrogen (Bosch process) or for synthesizing methyl alcohol. Usually producer gas and water gas are mixed because it is much more economical to alternate the exothermic and endothermic reactions; this is colloquially known as 'blow and run'.

Typical raw materials for gas production are hogged wood, wood refuse, bark, tannery refuse, and sawdust. Non-forest sources of organic waste can also be gasified; for example, olive refuse, bagasse, cotton-seed husk, rice husk, sunflower-seed husk, cashew-nut shell, ground-nut husk, coconut shell, corn cob, grape seed, and coffee grounds. Producer-gas units offer an almost perfect answer for countries that are short of fossil fuel but have ample carbonaceous waste materials. Dual-fuel internal combustion engines have been designed to cope with situations where supply of a particular waste is seasonal or liable to fluctuation. They can operate on gas or oil or a mixture of both in any proportion, without having to stop to change over from one fuel to another.

Fuels with moisture contents up to 50 per cent may be used but as with the production of energy from fuelwood it is an advantage to reduce the moisture content to 30 per cent or less for best results. Some examples of producer-gas plants in operation are given in Table 3.8.

TABLE 3.8
Producer gas plants in current use at various locations

Country	Power output (b.h.p.)	Fuel	Output (m^3 gas/h)
England	125	Sawdust	n.a.
Kenya	350	Logs	710
Sri Lanka	75	Wood blocks 10 X 10 X 10 cm	n.a.
Portugal	350	Wood blocks 15 X 10 X 10 cm	700
India (Travancore)	6000	Logs	in 6 units 21 240
West Africa	1000	Logs	2000
South Africa	350	Wood blocks of max. size 30 X 10 cm	710

Source: Davy Power Gas Ltd. (1969)

The ash from the producer plants may be sold to farmers or foresters as a fertilizer for returning trace elements to the soil, as is done in India. In large-scale gas production for heating, for power purposes, and for use in chemical process plants, where the bulk density of the fuel is relatively unimportant, it is far cheaper to use a primary fuel source; but for more sophisticated use, such as in transport where the fuel has to be carried, charcoal is more economical.

Charcoal, because of its high carbon content, is an ideal fuel for the generation of producer gas for internal combustion engines used in vehicles, as has been successfully demonstrated in many countries during times of oil shortage. The charcoal should have a low volatile content to prevent gumming-up of the engine and should be dense, or briquetted if possible, to cut down bulk.

Producer units are usually arranged so that water can be sprayed on to the charcoal to prevent over-heating and this arrangement has the advantage of adding water gas to the fuel available. The producer units are usually rather heavy (100 kg minimum) and therefore they are much more suitable for buses and lorries than for private cars. A tonne of charcoal is equivalent to 720 litres of petrol under normal running conditions and it is therefore clear that producer gas plants for heavy transport in countries with cheap available charcoal are not only technically feasible but likely to be much more economically and socially accept-able than traditional forms of transport requiring imported petroleum.

The principal types of vehicles that have been run successfully on producer gas are lorries, tractors, cars, and buses. In Sweden the state railways operated more than 100 trains with producer gas in 1941 (Kissin 1942) and this would appear to be an excellent area for development in countries with adequate raw materials for charcoal.

Hydrogen from wood may well become the transport fuel of the future in economies where the basic energy supplies are obtained from nuclear power. It is extremely difficult and therefore expensive to extract hydrogen from electroly-sis of water on a large scale. The hydrogen contained in wood cellulose could be obtained chemically at a fraction of the cost by using waste heat from power stations and a suitable catalyst.

The use of wood as fuel in power stations
Electrical energy is very expensive to produce compared with energy supplied directly from fuels but it has very many advantages which could make it desir-able to convert wood energy to electricity in areas where the supply of wood is not limiting.

A power station of reasonable size would be 150 megawatt, requiring a raw material input of approximately 786 600 cubic metres of air-dried wood per annum.The forest area needed to sustain production would depend upon the amount of wood residues available and on the increment from natural forest or energy plantations. It could well lead to a new concept of forest management which might be concerned to maximize production of biomass irrespective of timber quality, or to a resurrection of old techniques of forest craft such as coppice with standards (the latter providing timber and other benefits).

An example of the calculation of the forest area needed to sustain such a power station is as follows.

1. Banyankole earth kiln—Mabira, Uganda. Production is about 1½ tonnes per man per month

2. Group of portable steel kilns—Lwamunda, Uganda. Each kiln produces 6 tonnes of charcoal per month

3. Group of Missouri kilns—USA. Each kiln produces about 40 tonnes of charcoal per month

Assumptions:
  (1) The air-dried wood yields 3.5×10^6 kcal–tonne.
  (2) The thermal–electric conversion is 35 per cent.
  (3) The power station runs at 60 per cent efficiency.
  (4) The increment of fuelwood, i.e. stems and branches including bark is
      20 cubic metres per hectare per annum.
  1 tonne wood at 35 per cent conversion = 1420 kilowatt-hours
  1 megawatt (year) = 8.76×10^6 kilowatt-hours
  1 megawatt requires $\dfrac{8.76 \times 10^6}{1420}$ = 6169 tonnes wood
  150 megawatts at 60 per cent load = 90 megawatts
  Therefore wood required $\widehat{=}$ 560 000 tonnes
                          = 773 000 cubic metres
  Forest area to sustain wood supply = 38 650 hectares

With the total utilization concept embodied in a project of this type, it should be comparatively easy to arrange for the ash residues in the furnaces to be returned to the forest, thus reducing the need for inputs of calcium, potash, and trace elements.

A report, *The U.S. energy problem*, prepared by the Intertechnology Corporation for the National Science Foundation (1973), suggests that the establishment of 'energy plantations' in the U.S.A. equivalent to one-seventh of the U.S. forest area would satisfy the entire U.S.A. budget. The wood produced by quick-growing trees would be converted to electricity in local power stations.

Uhart (1971) suggests that in clearing operations in the Amazon, the gas obtained from retorts converting wood to charcoal could be used to generate electricity. He makes the following calculations:

Wood production per ha	250 m³ or 200 tonnes
Calorie content of 200 tonnes wood at 3·0 kcal/g	600 000 000 kcal
Lambiotte retort production	50 tonnes charcoal and 30 000 m³ gas

Energy production:		
	charcoal	350 000 000 kcal
	electrical (from gas)	11 610 000 kcal
	Total	361 610 000 kcal or 52 tonnes CE
Efficiency of conversion		60·3 per cent

A much cheaper and simpler retort than the Lambiotte has been designed by de Lacotte at Rans in the Jura area of France. The Lacotte process utilizes about 20 tonnes of waste wood per day from which 4–5 tonnes of charcoal and enough gas to power an engine generating electricity at the rate of 450 kWh are obtained. This unit would be particularly valuable for operation at sawmills in remote areas as it would allow very efficient equipment to be used at very low cost.

4 The potential for supplying renewable energy from forests

'The forest is a peculiar organism of unlimited
Kindness and benevolence that makes no demands
For its sustenance and extends generously
The products of its life activity; it affords
Protection to all beings, offering shade even
To the axeman who destroys it.'
Gautama Buddha

The renewability of forest energy

Wood is a renewable fuel resource because energy removed from the forest capital stock can be replaced by recruitment of solar power for synthesis of new material. Photosynthesis is an endothermic chemical process leading to the formation of carbohydrate; it may be represented by the following much-simplified equation:

$$CO_2 + H_2O + 112 \cdot 3 \text{ kcal} \longrightarrow (CH_2O) + O_2.$$

Although imbalance of water or nutrients or some other factors, singly or in combination, may inhibit the growth of vegetation and there may be insufficient thermal energy for plant growth at the polar extremes and on some of the highest mountain ranges, there is enough light for growth to take place at any latitude. Fig. 4.1 shows the estimated annual fixation of carbon for the land surface of the earth. According to Sukachev and Dylis (1964), the principal factor that limits the rate of photosynthesis in terrestrial plants is shortage of carbon dioxide in the atmosphere. Under localized conditions where light is the limiting factor, provided that the carbon dioxide concentration is high, approximately 540 kcal of light energy are required to store 105 kcal of chemical energy (Helmers and Bonner 1959). Photosynthesis is therefore approximately 21 per cent efficient, but because only about 25 per cent of the incident light energy is available for photosynthesis, the rest being converted to heat and wasted, the theoretical overall efficiency of a forest should be $0 \cdot 25 \times 0 \cdot 21 = 0 \cdot 05$ or 5 per cent, as has been obtained for crops grown in high carbon dioxide concentrations. The overall efficiency of a fully-stocked forest, because it is limited by the concentration of carbon dioxide, is normally of the order of 2 to $2 \cdot 5$ per cent.

The productivity of forests

The productivity of forests of various types and in different climatic regions has been the subject of much conjecture. From estimates of net primary production of carbon for different types of vegetation, Olson (1970) estimates that the total annual carbon fixed by the world's forests is about double that obtained with other forms of land-use, and the rate of accumulation of carbon per hectare for agricultural land is only half the rate for most forests, with the exception of those in the dry zones (Table 4.1).

TABLE 4.1

Estimates of net primary production of carbon fixed by the various major land ecosystems of the world

		Area (ha $\times 10^9$)	Net primary production (tonnes/ha)	Total annual production (tonnes $\times 10^9$)
Woodland or forest				
Temperate cold deciduous		0·8	10	8·0
Boreal conifer and mixed		1·5	6	9·0
Rain forest temperate		0·1	12	1·2
Rain forest tropical and sub-tropical		1·0	15	15·0
Dry woodlands (various)		1·4	2	2·8
	Total	4·8	av.7·5	Total 36·0
Non-forest				
Agricultural		1·5	4	6·0
Grassland		2·6	3	7·8
Tundra		1·2	1	1·2
Desert		3·2	1	3·2
Glacial		1·5	–	0·0
	Total	10·0	av. 1·8	Total 18·2

Source: Olson (1970)

The point is made by Kira, Ogawa, and Yoda (1957) that the natural forest ecosystem, with its stratified structure, seems more efficient at utilizing the available space and the radiant energy that falls upon it as compared with single-layered, widely spaced crop communities. It would appear to be reasonable to attribute part of the observed greater carbon assimilation rate of forest, as compared with agricultural crops, to the fact that there is a more frequent harvesting of crops from the latter, which would have the effect of reducing the time available for photosynthesis. Agricultural crops usually have quite heavy inputs of energy introduced by way of fertilizers, which are less frequently given to forests. The more intensive the silvicultural regimes, the more likely it is that soil deterioration will occur unless special attention is paid to fertility.

Natural forests are, for practical purposes, in a state of dynamic equilibrium in which losses from respiration and decay are made good by gains from photosynthesis. If a constraint is applied to the system, e.g. the removal of timber trees or a thinning operation, a change will take place within the system to oppose the constraint so applied and to restore the equilibrium c.f. Le Chatelier's Principle.

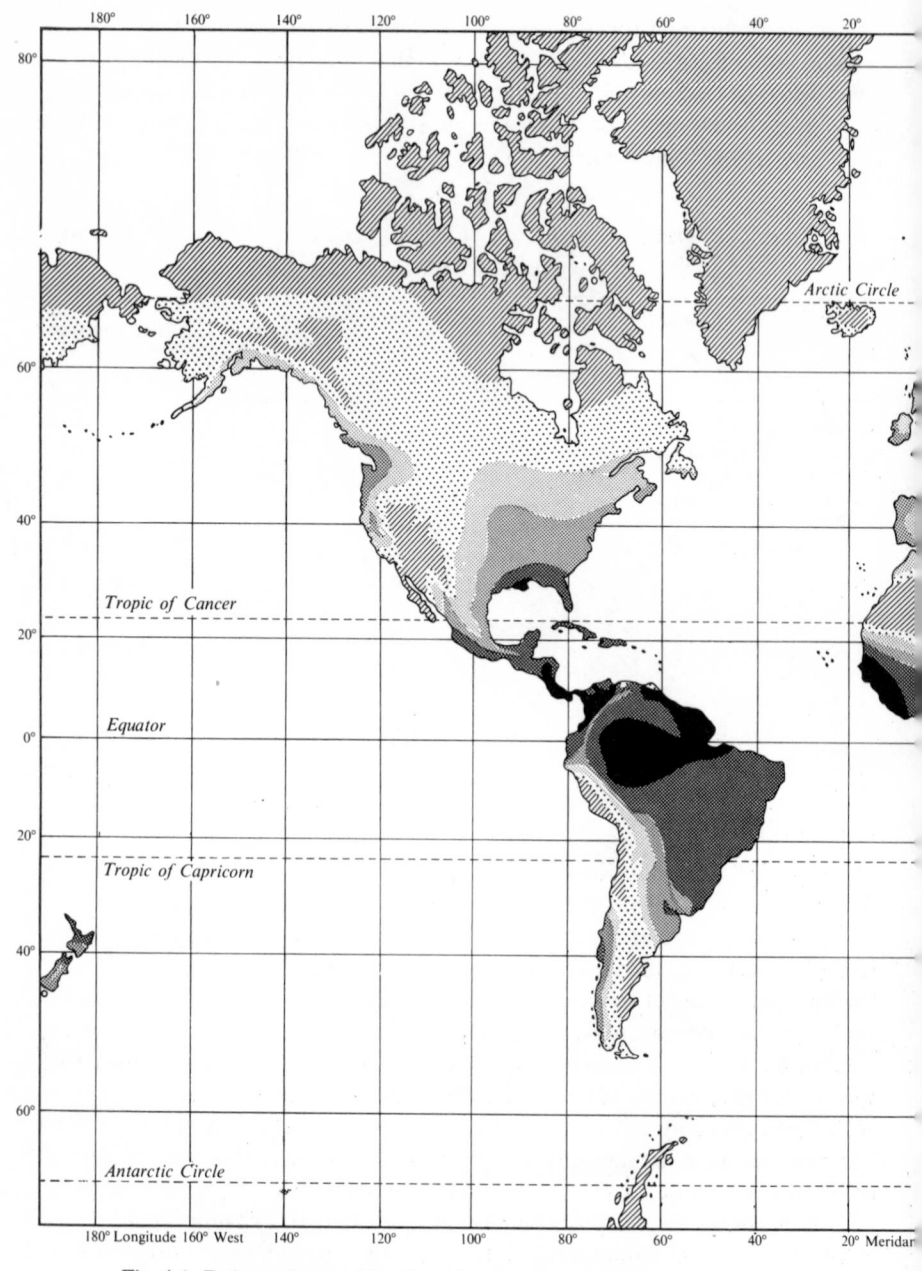

Fig. 4.1. Estimated annual fixation of carbon for land surface.
(After Lieth, H. (1972). In *Analysis of temperate forest ecosystems* (ed. Reichle, D.E.).
Chapman and Hall, London).

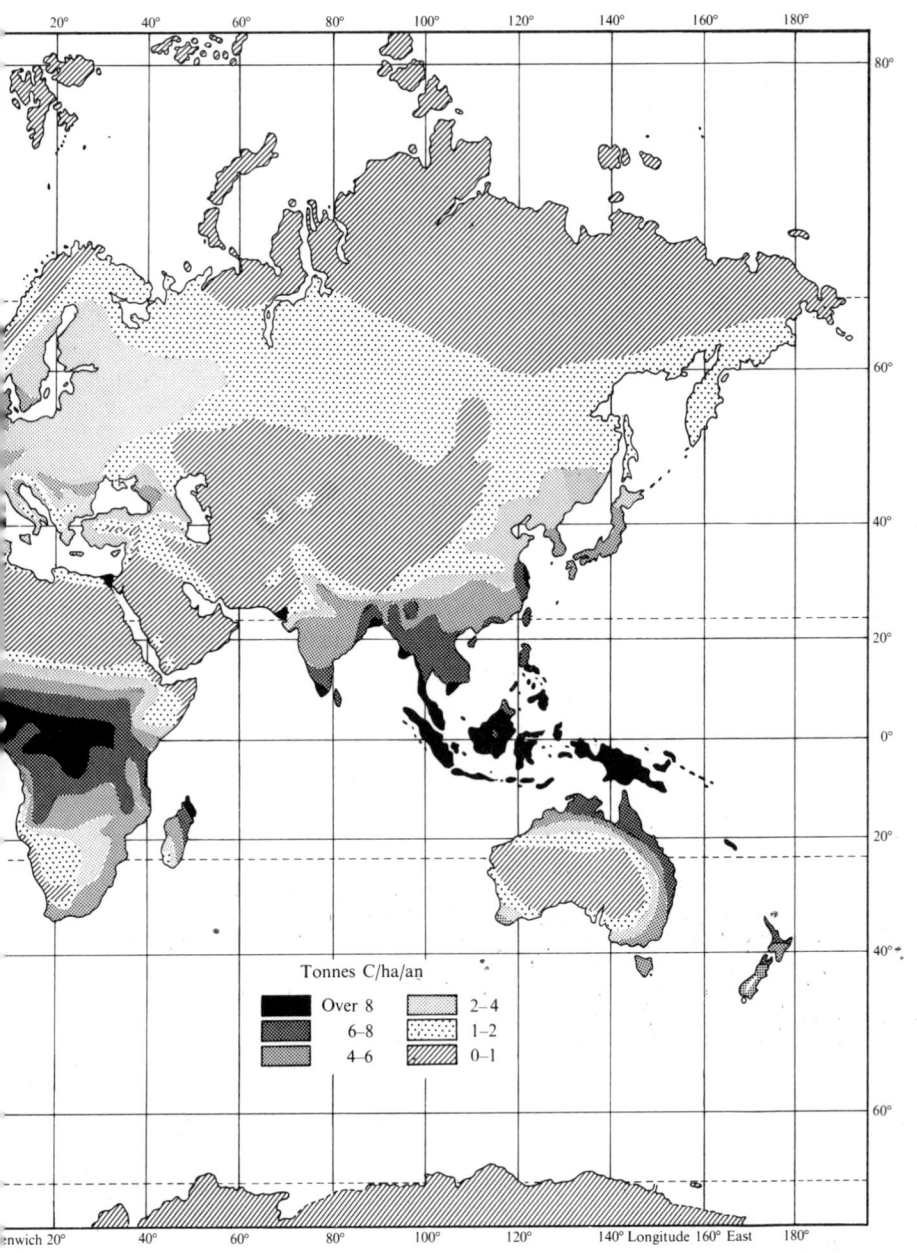

Tonnes C/ha/an

■ Over 8		2–4
6–8		1–2
4–6		0–1

There are difficulties in measuring the increment of dry matter produced by forests, and a certain amount of confusion arises because of different interpretations of what constitutes productive increment. Total gross primary production includes roots, leaves, and twigs, before losses caused by respiration are taken into account; net primary production excludes the latter. The range of estimates of maximum primary production in the tropics, from a number of sources, varies between 55–123 tonnes (oven dry weight) per hectare gross or 8–40 tonnes per hectare net above ground only. The upper limits of both ranges are somewhat lower in other climatic zones.

Foresters generally measure only stemwood, which may include branchwood, but occasionally estimates are for total above-ground primary production. Paterson (1956) developed a general index for estimating the potential productivity of stem wood in cubic metres per hectare using only climatic factors in his formula:

$$I = \frac{T_v \times P \times G \times E}{T_a \times 12 \times 100}$$

where T_v is the temperature of the warmest month (degrees Celsius), P is the annual rainfall (millimetres), G is the length of the growing season (months), E is the percentage reduction for evapo-transpiration, and T_a is the amplitude between mean hottest and mean coldest months. The index varies between $25–100 = 2\cdot1$ cubic metres per hectare, and $20\,000–30\,000 = 15\cdot6$ cubic metres per hectare.

Paterson's index, as revised by Weck (1957), was modified by Becking (1962), who produced a table in which he estimated that the total production in tonnes per hectare was greatest in the lowland tropics, but the percentage of stem-wood to total production was lowest; see Table 4.2.

TABLE 4.2

Stemwood production in tonnes/ha of dry matter for different forest types

Forest type	Total production dry matter (tonnes/ha)	Stem-wood production (tonnes/ha) (Becking)	(Weck)	Percentage of stem-wood to total production (Becking)	(Weck)
THF lowland 0–500 m above sea level	63·0	13·2	8·8	21	14
THF 500–1500 m above sea level	54·6	11·5	7·6	21	14
Temperate rain forest	31·0	9·3	9·3	30	30
West European forest	18·0	5·8	5·8	32	32

Source: Becking (1962)

Various estimates indicating that net productivity is not much greater in the tropical zone than it is in the temperate zone have been given by Rodin and Basilvec (1967), Kira (1969), and Wycherley and Templeton (1969).

Potential productivity is undoubtedly greater in the tropics than in the temperate regions, as has been proved by the high yields obtained from managed forests and exotic species. Figures of maximum dry weight above-ground production of 17 tonnes per hectare per annum for tropical high forest on lowland sites and 40 tonnes for Eucalyptus at more than 100 metres above sea level were given by Dawkins in an unpublished thesis (1964), who estimated that the range of widely practicable production of total above-ground stem wood of tropical hardwoods from first-quality sites is 6–12 tonnes dry weight per hectare per annum. The explanation for the apparent low yield of tropical forests as compared with temperate forests is that not only is the proportion of usable stem wood lower but the loss through respiration and biological deterioration is very much higher in the tropics. It would appear that although productivity of tropical high forest is higher than that of temperate woodlands, it is lower than most people would assume from a cursory examination of the biomass.

The extent of the world's forest energy resource
Estimates of the earth's total land area vary but the most commonly quoted figure is 14 900 million hectares, which includes Antarctica (1300 million ha) and inland water (400 million ha). The area of the earth covered with forest is variously estimated as 5700 million hectares (Lieth 1972); 4800 million hectares (Olson 1970); and 3800 million hectares (F.A.O. 1972). These estimates are necessarily approximate because of the difficulty in defining exactly what constitutes forest in many parts of the globe. The F.A.O. (1966a) figure, which is based on country returns submitted for the *World forestry inventory 1963*, is probably conservative, for it refers only to forest lands reserved as such by the governments concerned. It is estimated that energy equivalent to 271 000 million tonnes of coal is contained in the growing stock of the world's forests. The classification of forest types employed in the *Oxford economic atlas of the world* (1972) see Fig. 4.2, has been used, with relevant area, productivity and utilization data to make an estimate of the rate of renewal and removal of the solar energy store contained in the world's forest resource (see Tables 4.3 and 4.4).

From Table 4.4, it can be seen that only 13 per cent of the world's forest increment is at the present time (1970) being harvested, 7 per cent for industrial purposes and 6 per cent as fuel. Of the world's forest increment, 51 per cent, i.e. 9000 million cubic metres, is produced in the tropical developing countries, of this only 11 per cent, i.e. 1000 million cubic metres, is at present being utilized (2 per cent for industry and 9 per cent for fuel). In terms of coal equivalents there is a loss each year of 3500 million tonnes in the developing world. Much of this

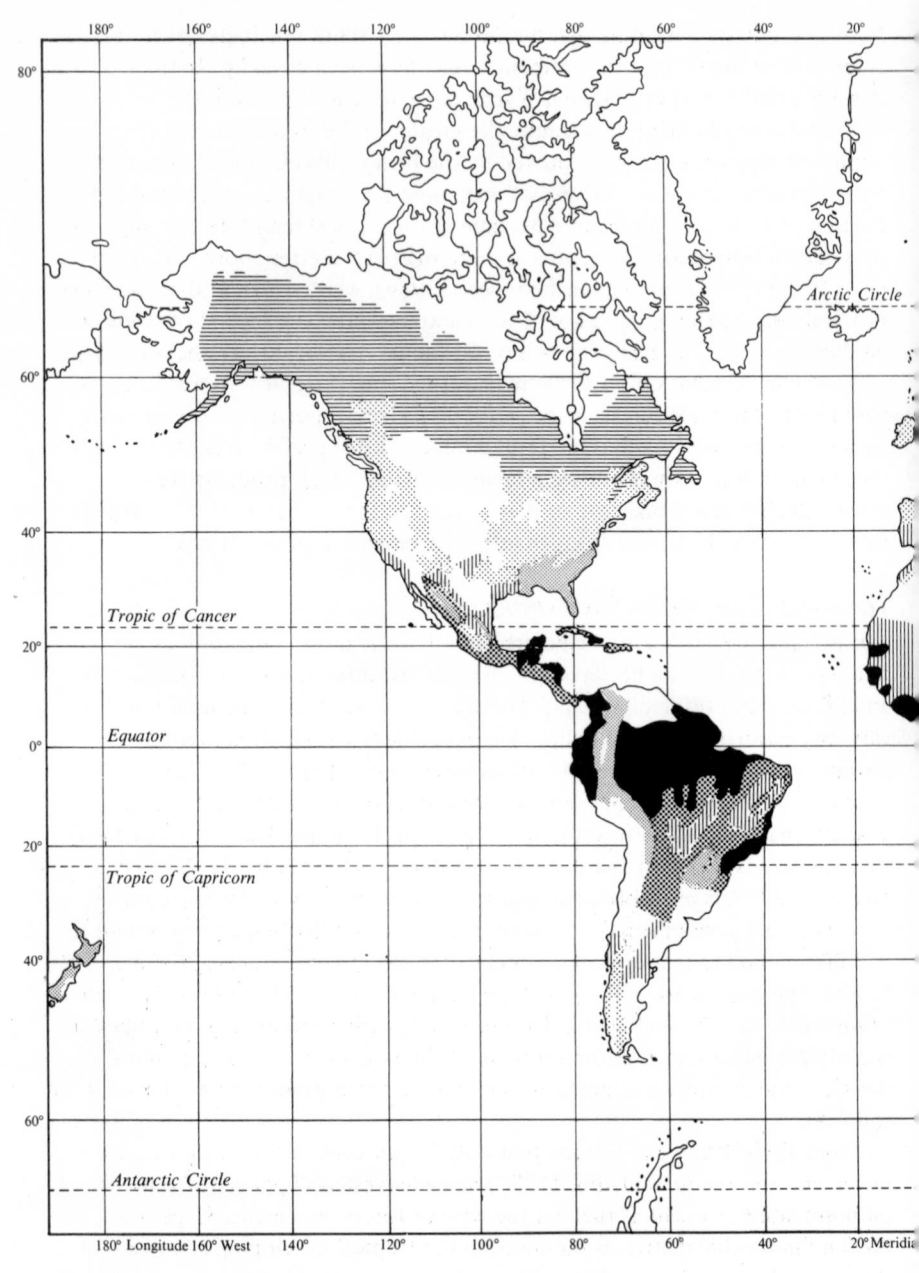

Fig. 4.2. The world's forests.

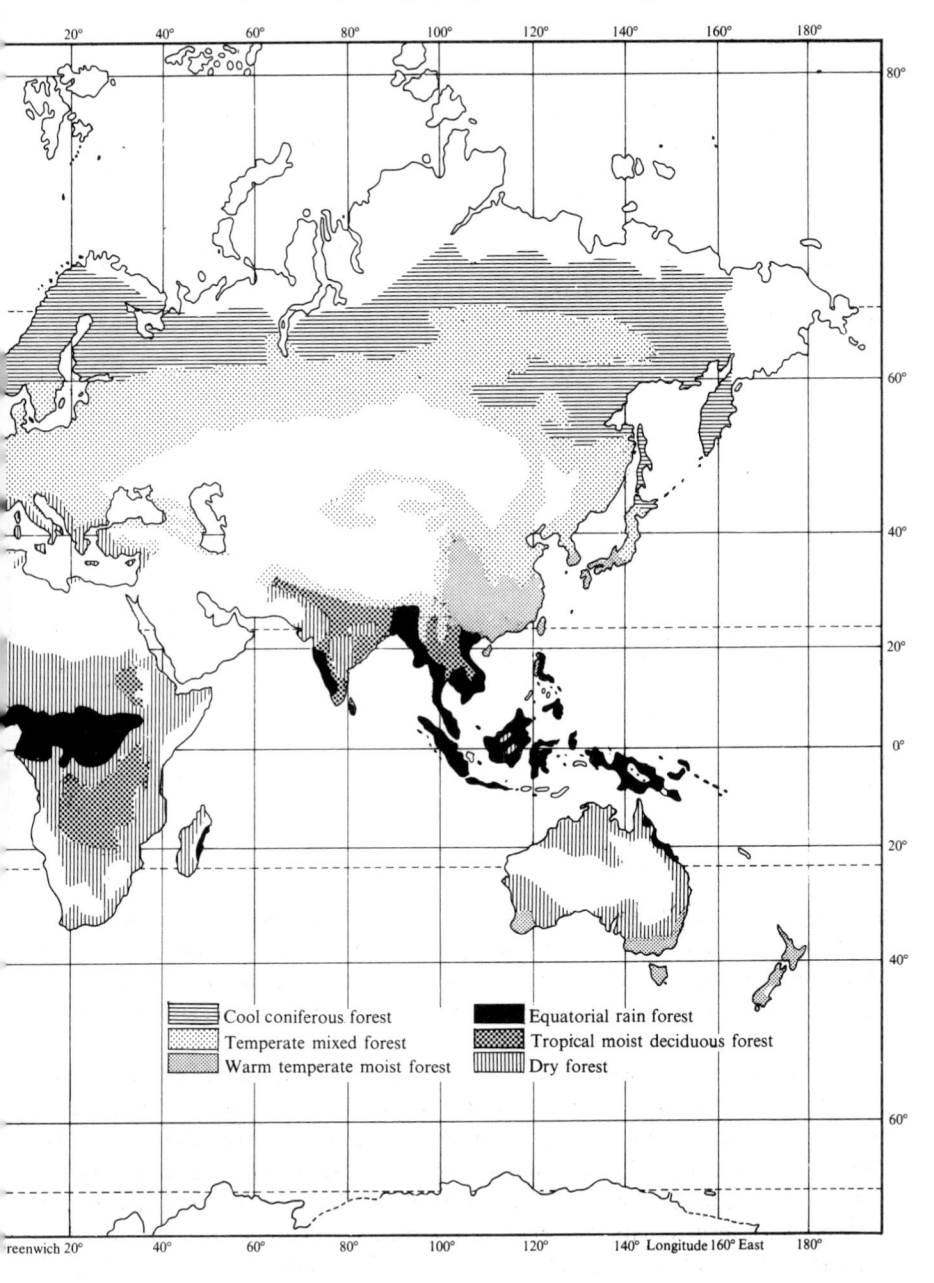

Cool coniferous forest
Temperate mixed forest
Warm temperate moist forest
Equatorial rain forest
Tropical moist deciduous forest
Dry forest

TABLE 4.3

The world's renewable forest energy resource

Forest type	Area (ha X 10⁶)	Annual increment of wood† per ha (m³)	(tonnes)	Total increment wood† (m³ X 10⁹)	(tonnes X 10⁹)	(tonnes CE X 10⁹)
Cool coniferous	800	4·1	3·0	3·3	2·4	1·4
Temperate mixed	800	5·5	4·0	4·4	3·2	1·9
Warm temperate	200	5·5	4·0	1·1	0·8	0·5
Equatorial rain	500	8·3	6·0	4·1	3·0	1·8
Tropical moist deciduous	500	6·9	5·0	3·5	2·5	1·5
Dry	1000	1·4	1·0	1·4	1·0	0·6
Totals and means	3800	4·7	3·4	17·8	12·9	7·7

† Estimated to include all wood above ground.

TABLE 4.4

The utilization of the world's incremental forest energy resource (1970)

	Growing stock† (m³ X 10⁹)	Increment (m³ X 10⁹)	Used for industrial purposes (m³ X 10⁹)	Used for fuel (m³ X 10⁹)	Total consumption (m³ X 10⁹)	Unused increment (m³ X 10⁹)	Unused increment (tonnes CE X 10⁹)
Developed countries	242	8·8	1·1	0·3	1·4	7·4	3·2
Developing countries	382	9·0	0·2	0·8	1·0	8·0	3·5
Total	624	17·8	1·3	1·1	2·4	15·4	6·7

† Estimated to include all wood above ground

increment, if removed from overstocked forests by silviculturally sound techniques, would serve to increase the increment rate of the remaining more valuable trees. This is an important consideration if the demand for wood products is likely to increase at a faster rate than hitherto because of the expected increase in price of alternative resources.

The estimated percentage of increment removed from the world's forest estate of 3800 million hectares (assuming that it remains the same size) on the basis of the extrapolation of present trends will probably increase to 19 per cent in 1985. The demand for fuelwood is likely to remain inelastic, as opposed to the demand for industrial wood which is highly elastic at the income levels of developing countries. We can therefore postulate that the forest resource is theoretically large enough to cater for human energy needs without affecting the supply of wood for industrial purposes, provided that the silvicultural systems are adapted to the production of fuelwood together with the production of timber. The distribution and accessibility of the forest areas in relation to fossil fuel deposits and human populations, however, will determine whether or not the provision of forest energy is economic. Severe competition for space in regions with high populations may imply continued necessary dependence upon fossil energy resources and future nuclear supplies, but even in these areas the optimum 'mix' of land allocated for different purposes might well include a provision for fuelwood plantations as part of a strategy aimed at achieving a better ecological balance; this strategy would include positive steps to reduce the human population density.

The potential of the tropical forest energy resource

Natural forests, in dynamic equilibrium, are able to balance energy gains against losses. Silviculturists may apply a constraint to the equilibrium situation by the removal of harvestable increment under controlled conditions to accelerate the photosynthetic process.

The tropical high forest is characterized by its extreme diversity: it is not uncommon to harvest in one forest more than one hundred tree species with an enormous range of morphological and timber properties giving rise to many economic and technical problems for the exploiting agency. The potential increment of tropical forest can be increased, beyond that obtainable by removal of the theoretical increment of natural gain, by selective removal of slow-grown and moribund stock, followed by enrichment with fast-growing species or by conversion to plantations.

The advantages of plantations are well-known but a summary of the main points given by Logan (1965) is shown below.

(1) Plantations allow close control of the nature and quality of the wood raw material, and yield a crop of which a high proportion of the woody growth is harvestable, thus enabling the silvicultural work to be carried out to suit the objects of management.

(2) Increments of more than 50 cubic metres per hectare per annum have been obtained from Eucalyptus fuelwood plantations over short rotations (6—8 years) in Africa under exceptionally good site conditions. More representative figures are 20—70 cubic metres per hectare per annum in South America and 15—25 in tropical Africa. On drier sites the increment might well be below 10 cubic metres per hectare per annum. Selected species in the tropical natural forest may match these growth rates but the average increment of the useful species is considerably less.

(3) The homogeneous nature of the crop and the fast rates of growth achievable by quick-growing plantations provide very high out-turns of harvestable wood per hectare. In consequence, substantially smaller areas of land need to be used for wood production. This may be of great advantage in countries which are short of land for food production or settlement; it also reduces the costs of protection and supervision. In harvesting, too, the high out-turns per hectare and uniform nature of the crop make for lower costs per unit of wood extracted.

(4) Provided that suitable land is available, plantations give management the opportunity to site its raw material source and processing plant to the best advantage, economically, in relation to markets and to each other.

(5) Under favourable conditions, quick-growing plantations can be profitable financial undertakings.

In financial terms it is sometimes difficult to justify timber-growing as an investment because the return may be less than the interest charge required for the large input of capital needed at the early part of a long rotation. In the northern hemisphere it is thought that forests established on good sites, with average expenditure on ground preparation and planting, earn about 3 per cent on the invested capital. Over a 35-year rotation this is equivalent to 2·8 times the initial investment if the annual maintenance costs and the costs and returns from thinnings are excluded. If, however, the opportunity cost of capital were 5 per cent, safe alternative investment would be expected to yield 5·5 times the initial investment over the same period. If the opportunity cost of capital were 10 per cent, a yield expectation of 28·1 times the sum invested would be necessary after 35 years to equal the returns expected from alternative investment. The effect of compound interest upon the attractiveness of forestry as an investment is not always understood sufficiently well by foresters, who sometimes perform costly operations which could not possibly lead to an increase in the subsequent return from the forest big enough to justify the extra interest charges incurred.

In developing countries plantations can be established much more cheaply than in developed countries because of the low cost of operations with an essentially high labour content. Logan (1965) reports that plantations in Indonesia capable of yielding 25 cubic metres per hectare per annum can be established for about one-tenth of the average cost in developed countries. The establishment of plantations is not always the panacea for difficulties in supplying fuelwood to towns and industry. There are a number of reasons for this, including the risks of losses from insects, fires, and other calamities to which plantations are more prone than mixed natural forests.

Attention has recently been centred upon the growing importance of tropical forests in preservation of the global environment, and it is feared by some environmentalists that conversion of these forests to other forms of land-use might have global repercussions affecting the carbon dioxide budget, the thermal balance, and the climate. The natural forests provide a habitat for the wildlife which constitutes an important source of food for a large number of nomadic people. These forests protect and conserve the fragile tropical soils and prevent erosion, drought, and deterioration of water quality. With growing urbanization the forests provide recreational facilities for the people and may be an integral part of the attractions offered by a country to foreign visitors. It is unknown whether or not the tree species grown today will be the only ones useful to man in the future, and it would therefore be presumptuous to conclude that because many of the trees in tropical forests have only a low value under present market conditions this will always be so. Geneticists, too, are worried lest potentially valuable strains may be eliminated with consequent loss to the gene bank. Although economies of scale suggest that homogeneous crops are more financially desirable than mixed forests, it is reasonable to consider the possible undesirable externalities which might arise and attempt to make contingency plans accordingly.

The potential for increasing the supply of forest fuel at minimum cost

Fortunately, it is not always necessary to convert natural forests to plantations in order to maximize the potential financial return. In many parts of the world the population pressure, although increasing, is not at the point where every piece of of the forest land resource has to be directed to producing the maximum return per hectare. The problem is one of obtaining maximum return on capital expenditure without losing the many other diverse benefits, including those that are unquantifiable and intangible, provided by the forests. The financial return from plantations is not necessarily greater than from managed mixed forests where the marginal efficiency of the land factor is greater than that of the other factor inputs. Refining and enrichment, rather than replanting tropical high forest can sometimes not only maximize return on capital but can also provide an optimum mix of social and consumer goods, e.g. fuel and timber (Earl 1972b). The financial return from forests of this type is generally higher than can be expected from plantations because of the higher marginal product of capital from land-extensive rather than from land-intensive schemes. The case for providing fuel plantations near to population centres where land pressure is highest depends very much upon the opportunity cost of land, and this may result in a trade-off between food and fuel production. The extensive treatment of natural forest is complementary to intensive plantation establishment if the maximization of environmental, financial, and social benefits from the forest resource is embodied in the management policy. The benefit to a country from a policy which seeks to maximize use of forest energy lies not only in the increased share of profits which may accrue from the fuller utilization of forest produce but also in the savings in silvicultural costs which may be obtained in consequence. The decision on which type of treatment is applicable to any particular forest should be made only after suitable analysis using economic and ecological criteria.

If forests grow on publicly-owned land with an opportunity cost, it is reasonable to expect the resource to be managed to provide the best net social benefit for the nation concerned. This will include studying the needs of the local people. The importance of studying the full implications of decisions leading to a change in the character of the forest must be stressed, for a change on commercial grounds may not necessarily be to the advantage of the local people who depend upon the forest for their livelihood.

Fuel production can be organized so as to provide the means of managing either extensive or intensive forests profitably. If not organized, it can lead to a reduction of net social benefit by the loss of forests altogether. Four typical situations in which fuel production can improve the economic returns from the forest resource are now discussed briefly.

The conversion and refining of tropical high forests. Tropical high forests are often poorly or incompletely exploited for timber. Although the range of sizes and species of merchantable trees is becoming extended with time, in some countries as little as 2 per cent of the forest growth ever contributes anything to the GNP. The process of exploitation also commonly causes such havoc in the forest that the damage can be rectified only by operations costing more than the royalties received from the sawmillers. Some foresters, e.g. Wyatt Smith (1968), recommend the abandonment of management in tropical high forests and suggest that the money available for forestry would be better spent on the creation of plantations. One of Wyatt Smith's main points is that it is difficult to prevent theft from tropical high forest, whereas everyone knows that a plantation has been created as a deliberate act and is therefore not a free social good to be taken without permission. Others, e.g. Gane (1966) and Earl (1968), think that there is a tendency for foresters to regard the management of tropical high forest as an inferior form of silviculture as compared with the establishment and management of plantations, and they consider that more attention should be paid to the care of this very important resource. Where, however, there are abundant forests and at the same time potential for the increased use of fuel, there is the opportunity of improving the economic status of forests at minimum cost by obtaining the benefits of increased utilization and, in addition, creating suitable conditions for the commencement of a more productive growth cycle. This opportunity is there because fuel, which can be obtained from any species or part of a tree or shrub without regard to its size or shape, can be harvested concurrently with the main timber operation in order to increase the revenue, and the removal of the fuelwood can be combined with operations aimed at increasing the stocking of desirable species.

Most of the early attempts to increase the productivity of tropical forests concentrated either on encouraging natural regeneration and growth of desirable species by poisoning unwanted competitors (e.g. Malaysian Shelter Wood System) or on planting the desired timber species in the natural forest in cleared or poisoned forest (*'Méthode du Recru'*) or in cleared lines in the forest (e.g. *'Méthode Sous-Bois'*). Most of these schemes have failed on economic grounds because of the high cost of clearing, cutting lines, poisoning, and maintaining the forest. With suitable attention to the market and to all benefits and costs, much of the wood that would have been destined to be cut, poisoned, and burned under these régimes can now more profitably be sold as fuel or charcoal. Apart from the obvious advantage of having the forest cleared of all growth at little or no cost before re-planting, there is the possibility of refining the forests.

Refining is the name for cleaning and thinning natural forests with the object of increasing the proportion of potential final crop timber trees in the stand. In the U.S.A., the expression 'timber stand improvement' (TSI) is synonymous with refining. Refining is flexible and adaptable to change and is thus less likely than conversion to plantations to result in irreversible environmental damage. For example, in addition to known timber trees it is easy to arrange to leave a proportion of non-timber trees for aesthetic reasons, for the provision of food for a particular class of animal or bird, or because it is felt that caution should be exercised in interfering too drastically with the natural balance.

In refining, some potential timber increment may be sacrificed in return for a low risk of environmental damage. Despite this fact, refining is often the most profitable management option for large forests because of the small financial inputs per treated unit area. The increment of timber, which is often only 1−2 cubic metres per hectare per annum, can easily be increased several-fold if refining is followed by enrichment. The silvicultural and economic justification for refining and enrichment in the tropics has been discussed by Moore (1957) and Earl (1968, 1972b). Refining can be carried out with arboricides, but this is more expensive and less environmentally desirable than selective removal of the trees and vegetation, unwanted for timber, for use as fuelwood and charcoal. If charcoal-making is done on site, there is the marketing advantage of concentrating the raw material to 25 per cent of its former weight and the silvicultural advantage of having sites suitable for enrichment prepared free of charge (Plate 5).

The conversion of unproductive, temperate, mixed woodland to more productive use. Of special interest to temperate countries is the rehabilitation of unproductive woodlands, i.e. areas of scrub, unworked coppice, or forest degraded through selective fellings of timber trees.

In the United Kingdom there are over 280 000 hectares of forest that are described as being covered with unutilizable scrub (Locke 1970). Many attempts have been made to deal with woodland of this type. All have involved high inputs of capital for the purchase of heavy clearing equipment or arboricides and very little effort has been directed at developing the market for the low-grade timber which could so easily be converted into charcoal.[†] One explanation for the paradox is that the Forestry Commission is concerned mainly with the production of timber raw material and very little with the development of markets. Marketing is left to private entrepreneurs who work to a profit motive in isolation from wider issues. Cheap oil products and dear labour have had the effect of pricing charcoal above the level of comparable fuels. It is clear that a cost−benefit analysis covering the effects on the community as a whole would show that it would be beneficial to pay the charcoal manufacturers a royalty for each tonne of charcoal produced, which could be used to reduce the retail price and thus make it more competitive with imported alternative fuel. Provided that the Forestry Commission were able to get the woodlands rehabilitated more cost-effectively even when bonuses were paid to charcoal makers, the method suggested would provide a bigger

† The U.K. is a net importer of charcoal. For example, in 1971 9589 tonnes of wood charcoal (valued at U.S. $1 140 000) and 3337 tonnes of activated charcoal (valued at U.S. $1 485 000) were imported.

return on capital invested in the forest operation as a whole. If the scrub contains trees of economic importance the overall return from the capital expended on these woodlands can be greater than that expended on plantation schemes if the only real economic constraint is the opportunity cost of the capital available. It is worth remembering that existing trees, even if they are not the most valuable or fast-growing species, will not incur establishment costs as sunk costs have no part to play in an economic appraisal. It might be more economic to practise cheap, extensive rehabilitation rather than to spend money on intensive conversion of a very small fraction of the area. The question asked should not be how to eradicate the existing woodland and replace it with another crop but how much of the existing woodland can be preserved and encouraged to grow into useful timber? Silvicultural objectives might be too narrow for present-day needs, and it is possible that different methods, such as coppice with standards, might produce the most gainful returns in hardwood areas. For example, the coppice would be converted to charcoal and the standards would provide timber and longer-term benefits. Any new approach should give much more flexibility to allow for ecological factors including human recreation; however, ecological factors should not be allowed to take preference over the necessity for making the country less dependent upon finite resources.

The opportunities for development of extensive forestry in Europe are smaller than those which exist in the tropics but nevertheless it is to be hoped that there will be some movement away from the belief that money spent on maximizing the return from a limited area of forest is better spent than a similar amount spread over a greater area of the same estate. The optimum benefits from forests can often be obtained more readily from mixed systems rather than monocultures.

Preparation of land for planting schemes. It sometimes may be necessary to clear away the cover of trees and bushes in order to convert land to some other use. Although it might appear to be cheaper to cut and burn or use arboricides, there is an even greater incentive to lower costs at the start of a new scheme, since any reduction made then will have the greatest effect in increasing the profitability of the project if economic criteria are to be used for the evaluation of its worth.

In the tropics even lightly-stocked savannahs can carry 8–20 tonnes of fuelwood per hectare, which may be either sold locally or converted to charcoal and transported to the nearest towns where it usually gives a profitable return to the producer as well as economic advantages to the silviculturist. If the clearing operation can be followed by *taungya* cultivation, then an appreciable saving in crop establishment costs will be secured. Investing authorities do not always realize that, as with the conversion of temperate woodland, it is often preferable to allocate money in order to help controlled fuel-cutting and charcoal-making become established rather than to spend money on heavy land-clearing equipment. Such help might include the provision of simple social amenities for the fuel-cutters and charcoal-makers, assistance in the organization of transport and markets, and

4. Two Lambiotte retorts used to convert waste Eucalyptus wood to charcoal, methyl alcohol, and acetic acid—Wundowie, Western Australia

5. Young crop of Musizi (*Maesopsis eminii*) two years after planting on a charcoal site

6. Forest destruction caused by shortage of cattle feedstuff
and fuel—Nepal

7. *Eucalyptus grandis* 5 years old, grown as fuel near
Kampala, Uganda

the provision of storage facilities by the government so that charcoal could be bought up at a guaranteed price during times of over-production and stored against time of fuel shortage.

Utilization of residues. The utilization of residues such as sawmill-waste, bark, and sawdust as fuel can be very important to the overall profitability of forestry, and for the entrepreneurs may make the difference between a successful business or insolvency. The impact upon the economics of forestry made by fuel marketed at the end of the rotation is less than that made by fuel marketed at the start because discounting reduces its financial worth appreciably. In developed countries with larger and more concentrated primary and secondary industries there are often good opportunities for cutting the losses on the disposal of materials such as bark and sawdust if they are converted to charcoal and briquetted; the ensuing value added more than covers the cost of conversion.

The future prospects for utilization of the world's forest energy sources

The world has an estimated forest growing stock equivalent to 271 000 million tonnes of coal, to which a potential increment of 7700 million tonnes of coal equivalent is added each year. The amount of increment obtainable depends upon the photosynthetic rate which, to some extent, is controllable by alteration of the environment, for example, by thinning. The art of silviculture lies in the organization of refining, thinning, and clearing operations so as to increase the amount of increment now, without decreasing the percentage of increment available in the future.

It is clear that the forests of the world are physically capable of producing and sustaining supplies of fuel well above the basic energy needs of man and that by application of improved silvicultural techniques they could produce very much more without affecting the supply of timber. In many developed countries the constraints upon the greater utilization of forests as a source of energy are principally economic, as most of the surplus increment is being generated in areas very remote from centres of industry which have grown up and flourished as a result of the availability of cheap, easily accessible fossil fuels.

In the developing world, however, under-utilized forests are frequently located in areas where economic and social development are desired and they thus present an opportunity for initiation of economic growth based on an indigenous energy resource. The development difficulty frequently lies not so much with economic considerations as with the technical and institutional constraints which favour the growth patterns set by the already industrially advanced countries.

5 The present consumption and future demand for forest energy

'The earth has enough for every man's need
but not for every man's greed.'
Mahatma Gandhi

Most countries have forest service organizations which collect statistics including the quantities of products removed from forests. These figures are submitted to the Forestry Section of the Food and Agriculture Organization, which publishes the details in its yearbook of forest products. These data vary in accuracy because forest produce which is removed from privately owned land or illegally from forest reserves often remains unrecorded. Probably the greatest quantity of unrecorded forest produce is removed for fuel. In Tanzania, Openshaw (1971) produced the startling fact that the recorded mainland production figure for fuelwood and charcoal for 1960 was less than 1·5 per cent of the estimated consumption figure determined by survey. It is the lack of complete information on present consumption which makes any study of the probable future demand for fuelwood much more difficult than forecasts of demand for other fuels. Recorded removals of fuelwood give a guide only to the minimum consumption of a country. Published figures which indicate a falling demand for fuelwood in some regions may sometimes point only to a decline in the efficiency of the forest authorities engaged in issuing licences. There are many interesting likely developments which might influence demand, for example, the production of producer gas, methanol, and charcoal briquettes of very high calorific value, which could revolutionize the economic status of those countries having extensive, untapped forest resources if the shortage of fossil fuel becomes acute. The bulk of present consumption is centred upon fuelwood and charcoal and it has to be assumed that any forecast of potential demand for forest energy will not be affected more than marginally by these more interesting speculations for some time to come.

The world's consumption of fuelwood and charcoal

The importance of wood as a primary energy source varies widely among different parts of the world. In Africa and Latin America 90 per cent of all wood used is for fuel and in Asia 65 per cent; but in Europe it is 25 per cent and in North America only 10 per cent. Table 5.1 shows the changes in recorded fuelwood production, including wood converted to charcoal, between 1951 and 1970.

TABLE 5.1
Change in recorded production of fuelwood
(including that converted to charcoal)

(a) 1951 to 1960

	Total production (million m³ solid)			Production *per capita* (m³ solid)		
	1951	1960	change 1951–60 (1951 = 100)	1951	1960	change 1951–60 (1951 = 100)
Europe	118	108	92	0·28	0·24	84
U.S.S.R.	108	101	93	0·59	0·46	79
N. America	67	46	69	0·40	0·23	58
Latin America	174	191	110	1·05	0·89	85
Africa	148	172	116	0·71	0·62	87
Asia Pacific	251	260	104	0·18	0·16	86
World Total	866	878	101	0·34	0·29	85

Source: F.A.O. (1966b)

(b) 1961 to 1970

	Total production (million m³ solid)			Production *per capita* (m³ solid)		
	1961	1970	change 1961–70 (1961 = 100)	1961	1970	change 1961–70 (1961 = 100)
Europe	91	62	68	0·20	0·13	65
U.S.S.R.	98	87	89	0·45	0·36	80
N. America	48	19	40	0·24	0·09	38
Latin America	188	223	119	0·88	0·80	91
Africa	208	255	123	0·75	0·73	97
Asia Pacific	397	475	120	0·24	0·23	96
World Total	1030	1121	109	0·34	0·31	91

Source: F.A.O. (1974).

The Yearbook of forest products 1972 (F.A.O. 1974) contains revised figures for the production of fuelwood from 1961, therefore an inter-tabular comparison between (a) and (b) above should not be made.

The figures indicate a decline in both total and *per capita* consumption of fuelwood in the developed countries, and an increase of more than 2 per cent in total consumption of fuelwood in the developing countries: *per capita* consumption in the developing countries, which declined 14 per cent in the 10 years 1951–60, decreased by only 4 per cent in the decade ending 1970. These changes can be partly attributed to more stringent measures taken in recording removals. The overall effect is a steady increase in the recorded consumption of fuelwood for the world of about 1 per cent per annum.

World charcoal production cannot be estimated with any degree of accuracy; many countries do not provide adequate statistics. The Food and Agriculture Organization's yearbooks of forest products include wood which is subsequently converted to charcoal in its estimates of fuelwood removals, but it is doubtful whether more than 18 million cubic metres of recorded fuelwood removed is currently converted to charcoal. There is a significant trend towards the use of charcoal in place of wood in the urban areas of developing countries but much charcoal manufacture is carried out by itinerants working for only part of the year and keeping no records of what they produce and sell. Even in developed economies the statistics of charcoal production are not always readily available and are often published in an *ad hoc* way. Efforts are being made to improve the recording of charcoal production in some countries where charcoal sections have been created within the Forest Department; for example, in Uganda each charcoal manufacturer is required to take out a licence based upon the amount of wood consumed per month. In this way the body most able to influence the activities of the charcoal industry is legally the focal point for the receipt of all statistical information. The system is not yet perfect but is moving towards the ideal of having a complete record of all wood removed and all charcoal produced.

Among the biggest producers of charcoal are those countries with large reserves of forests and well-developed industries requiring charcoal inputs. These countries include those listed below.

	Charcoal production (tonnes/annum)	
Brazil	1 000 000	(1969)
Malaysia	272 000	(1967)
Argentina	130 000	(1971)
France	90 000	(1965)

Japan is quite remarkable in that charcoal production has declined from an annual production of over 2 000 000 tonnes in 1950 to 361 000 tonnes in 1968. Charcoal was the principle fuel used for domestic cooking and heating until the Japanese economy grew strong enough to pay for imported fuel. This reliance upon imported fuel is putting Japan into a potentially dangerous economic position. The sudden cutting-off of oil supplies in the 1973 Arab–Israeli war showed how vulnerable the Japanese economy is to political influence affecting its imports. There are signs that unrestricted consumption of imported industrial feedstocks in Japan is associated with high social costs from pollution and an indication of this is the increased importation of coconut shell charcoal from Sri Lanka, to be activated for use in purification, especially of air and water.

Other countries which have well-developed domestic markets for charcoal are shown in Table 5.2. World trade in charcoal shows an overall upward trend. The most notable advance has been in Africa, where exports of charcoal have increased from 8000 tonnes in 1954 to 100 000 tonnes in 1969 valued at more than U.S.\$2 500 000 (F.A.O. 1970a). Some of the countries which have established good export markets for charcoal are shown in Table 5.3. There has been a

TABLE 5.2
Charcoal production for domestic purposes in selected countries

Country	Tonnes/annum	Year
U.S.A.	500 000	1969
Ghana	70 000	1970
Uganda	64 000	1972

Source: Forest Departments' records

TABLE 5.3
Charcoal exports for selected countries
(1970)

Country	Tonnes/annum
Somalia	48 000
Kenya	36 000
Roumania	28 000
Thailand	27 000
Germany	26 000
Sweden	21 000
Sri Lanka	20 000

Source: F.A.O. (1972)

remarkable increase in trade in activated carbon in the United Kingdom of which activated wood charcoal forms a significant part. If the United Kingdom is taken as being indicative of the trends in other industrial countries the extent of this new commercial interest can be gathered from the increase in exports of activated carbon from 1922 tonnes in 1962 to 24 036 tonnes in 1971.

F.A.O. data on recorded fuelwood removals are useful for indicating global trends in the use of forest energy, but for planning in individual regions or countries, estimates of actual consumption of fuelwood and charcoal for an area should be obtained by means of a consumer survey provided that the results are not extrapolated beyond the population concerned. Too often, estimates of consumption for whole regions or countries are based on figures obtained from too small a sample and with little attempt at achieving adequate coverage. Some lessons may be learnt from a number of estimates made of the fuel needs of the inhabitants of villages in the Bardia district of the Terai, Nepal (see Fig. 7.1).

The methodology used in carrying out the survey and the calculations of the present and future demand for fuel in the Terai and for the whole of Nepal based upon these surveys are described in Appendix 1.

The main points to emerge from these surveys are:

(1) The indigenous inhabitants of the Terai (the Tharu) use very much more fuelwood per household than immigrant people but because of the larger average family size, the *per capita* consumption of fuelwood by them is less than that of the other ethnic groups in the Terai.

(2) Hill people consume less fuelwood when living in their home areas, where it has a higher marginal utility than in the Terai, but soon begin to increase their consumption of fuelwood when they move to the Terai in conditions of abundance.

(3) The figures obtained from the different surveys indicate that there is wide variation in *per capita* consumption from village to village. Not too much reliance therefore should be placed on figures obtained from one village only, if general guidance on consumption is needed for an area.

(4) The F.A.O. figures based on Government returns of recorded removals are too low.

(5) Estimates based on consumption patterns for other countries can be gravely misleading.

General conclusion on estimates of fuel consumption

It is evident that the difference between recorded removals and consumption of fuelwood and charcoal, which may include unrecorded removals, should be determined before drawing any firm conclusions about trends in user habits. The figures for recorded removals should always be checked to see if all returns are being processed. F.A.O. yearbook figures, useful as they are, tend to be conservative; for example, the F.A.O. figure for recorded removals is shown by survey to be about 84 per cent of the total consumption of fuelwood in Nepal (in 1970).

Although available data on fuelwood consumption are derived only from recorded removals from forests and may lead to gross underestimates, some allowance must be made for the effects of more intensive agricultural and urban land-use upon the availability of 'free' fuel. As this 'free' fuel becomes scarcer, the need for fuel supplies from forests may be intensified.

Forecasting the demand for forest fuel

To be technically correct, demand (and supply) forecasts should be expressed in price—quantity relationships either as demand schedules, demand curves, or demand functions. A forest department planning for the supply of forest fuel should be more directly concerned with the probable future total energy consumption of the region, the predicted price of the alternative fuels, and the likely demand for forest fuel at a price high enough to justify making the investment. In practice the price factor is often assumed to follow existing trends and forecasts are based upon expected changes in population and real income (GNP *per capita*). Such forecasts may lead to conclusions which are patently false if the important effects of depletion and substitution upon price are ignored. Grayson (1972) bases his views that the annual increase in total consumption of fuelwood will probably level out from 1975 onwards, on a belief that costs of energy are likely to continue to fall. Runeburg (1972) considers that the capacity of timber for natural regeneration does not automatically give it an advantage over the plastics industry and extrapolates the fall in the price of plastics to a point well below the price of timber based on a belief in the inexhaustibility of cheap oil or of some alternative feedstock.

Population and real income *per capita* increases are obviously very important parameters. Furthermore, the abundant statistics available must be consulted before applying more sophisticated techniques.

Population increase

As shown in Table 5.4, the world population has been growing exponentially at a rate of 2 per cent per annum, i.e. 2·3 per cent in the developing countries and 1·4 per cent in the developed countries.

TABLE 5.4

World population growth 1920–68 projected to 2000 (in millions)

	1920	1930	1940	1950	1960	1968	2000	Percentage growth
Developed countries	662	742	801	834	952	1053	1388	1·4
Developing countries	1201	1328	1494	1683	2053	2520	4577	2·3
Total	1863	2070	2295	2517	3005	3573	5965	2·0

Based on data from F.A.O. (1966b), (1970b), and U.N. (1969).

The developing regions of Latin America, Asia, and Africa contain the largest populations with the highest growth rates and the countries with the lowest *per capita* incomes. In the developing countries the relationship between population growth rate and growth in fuelwood consumption is almost linearly related.

Real income per capita

Fig. 1.1 and Table 1.1, derived from U.N. statistics, show that GNP is correlated positively with energy consumption, but Fig. 5.1 indicates that although developing countries make greater use of forest fuel as compared with developed countries, GNP is not necessarily negatively correlated with consumption of forest fuel. Sweden with a *per capita* income of over U.S. $4000 has a *per capita* fuelwood consumption of 178 kilograms of CE, which is higher than that of many countries with far lower *per capita* GNP. Finland has the second highest *per capita* consumption of fuelwood on record and yet has a GNP *per capita* greater than that of the United Kingdom.

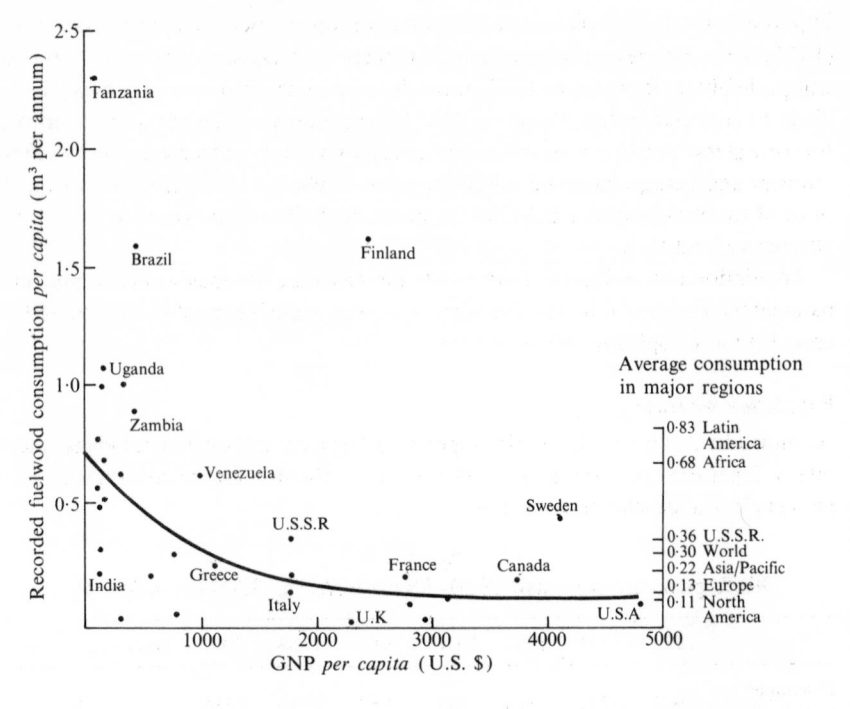

Fig. 5.1. Relationship between fuelwood consumption and GNP for selected countries.

There is an unmistakable trend for countries with the highest GNP *per capita* to be the largest users of commercial, non-renewable fuel but it is worth noting that the developing countries use much more energy from non-commercial, re-newable source such as agricultural waste, charcoal, dung, and fuelwood than do developed countries and that the low consumption of commercial energy for domestic use sometimes has less connection with the income of the inhabitants than with consumer preference for outdoor cooking with traditional fuels. For example, in Kathmandu, Nepal, coal is marginally cheaper than other fuels but the demand for it is negligible. The people prefer fuelwood, mainly Sal (*Shorea robusta*) which even with a government subsidy is dearer than coal. Increase in income in developing countries affects the consumption of fuelwood in two contrasting ways where it is associated with urbanization. The demand for fuelwood falls as consump-tion of electricity and fossil fuels increases. The consumption of fuelwood for conversion to charcoal increases as substitution of charcoal for fuelwood takes place.

The writer has found no evidence to show that energy consumption is related to climatic conditions. Although it might be expected that more fuel would be used for heating homes in cold climates, there are noticeable exceptions even in domestic economies; for example, traditionally, Eskimos survive with virtually no home heating. In market economies, too, there are heating peculiarities; for example, in the U.S.A. more energy is used for cooling houses in the summer than for heating them in winter. The conclusion must be reached that availability, consumer preference, and convenience of handling, as well as price are important points in favour of a particular fuel. These features are not confined only to developing economies. There is no justification whatsoever for assuming that energy from forest fuel sources is in any way inferior to that of any other fuel and every reason to encourage the expansion of the forest energy role where a comparative advantage can be gained.

The U.N. forecasts of world fuelwood demand

The F.A.O. has published three important works which include sections devoted to analysis of the projected production and consumption of fuelwood. *Wood: world trends and prospects* (F.A.O. 1966b) established the facts about the forestry sector's development to 1961 and went on to forecast its probable evolution to 1975. The study sought to provide reasoned guidelines for the policies and priorities for forest management in order to produce the type and quantity of wood that would be required, with the most rational use of available resources. The estimated growth of demand for wood products from the base years 1960–2 until 1975 was designed to give an indication of consumption (or requirements) when projected from the base year data under defined conditions and using the established trends in the development process.

The point was made in the *Provisional indicative world plan for agricultural development* (F.A.O. 1970b) that statistics for fuelwood are unreliable. This fact was emphasized in Table 5.5, which overstated the recorded consumption of fuelwood for 1962 and gave an estimate for 1975 which was less than the recorded removals for 1970 (see F.A.O. 1970b) and Table 5.6.

TABLE 5.5

Fuelwood: present and projected consumption and production

	1962	1975	1985
	$(m^3 \times 10^6)$	$(m^3 \times 10^6)$	$(m^3 \times 10^6)$
Developed countries	383	318	267
Developing countries	634	718	797
World total	1017	1036	1064

Source: *Provisional indicative world plan for agricultural development* F.A.O. (1970b)

TABLE 5.6

Fuelwood—past, present, and projected consumption ($m^3 \times 10^6$)

Region	1960[1]	1970[2]	1975[1]	1980[3]	Change 1960–70 (1960 = 100)
Europe	91	62	74	58	68
U.S.S.R.	98	87	80	82	89
N. America	48	19	34[5]	14	40
Latin America	188	223	220[5]	244	119
Africa	208	255	246	312	123
Asia Pacific	397	475	545	626	120
World	1030	1120	1199	1335	109

TABLE 5.7

Fuelwood—past, present, and projected per capita *consumption* (m^3)

Region	1960[1]	1970[4]	1975[4]	1980[4]	Change 1960–70 (1960 = 100)
Europe	0·20	0·13	0·12	0·10	65
U.S.S.R.	0·45	0·36	0·31	0·29	80
N. America	0·24	0·09	0·14[5]	0·05	38
Latin America	0·88	0·80	0·70[5]	0·72	91
Africa	0·75	0·73	0·63	0·66	97
Asia Pacific	0·24	0·23	0·25	0·27	96
World	0·34	0·31	0·30	0·30	91

[1] Source: *Wood: world trends and prospects* F.A.O. (1966b)
[2] Source: *Yearbook of forest products 1972* F.A.O. (1974)
[3] Source: *Agricultural commodity projections 1970–1980* F.A.O. (1971)
[4] Calculated by the writer from populations mid–1970, IBRD (1972), extrapolated at 1·4% for developed regions and 2·3% for developing regions
[5] It seems likely that Mexico (10 million m^3) was included in the North American total and excluded from Latin America.

Agricultural commodity projections 1970–80 (F.A.O. 1971) forecast a consumption of 1335 million cubic metres of wood as fuel in 1980. This figure is 15 per cent higher than the figure given in the F.A.O. (1966b) publication. The assumption was made, however, that there might be a shift in demand to other fuels in developing countries in response to demographic pressure upon regional fuelwood supplies. The F.A.O. projections to 1975 and 1980 used in Tables 5.6 and 5.7 indicate that there will continue to be a decline in the total and *per capita* consumption of fuelwood in developed countries. These tables also show that the gradual decline in *per capita* consumption in developing countries will come to an end and that their total and *per capita* consumption of fuelwood will increase. The net result will be that as more than 70 per cent of the world's population live in developing countries the total consumption of fuelwood for the world will increase and will represent in terms of volume, the largest section of all forest products.

Fuelwood demand trends in developing countries

It is in the developing countries where there is the greatest opportunity for making provision of forest fuel a major component of any land-use planning before the fuel problem becomes too great to handle (see Chapter 7). Some of these countries were, until recently, felt to be adequately endowed with forests but are now badly affected by a deteriorating fuel situation.

The National Commission on Agriculture for India (1972) reports that:

In respect of fuelwood, the picture is more alarming. Of the total consumption of $203^\dagger$ million m^3 of fuel only 13 million m^3 is said to come from the forest. It is assumed that the bulk of the fuelwood comes from treeslands but in actual fact this may include substantial pilferage from the forests. The fantastic demands for fuelwood in the future point towards the need for a planned provision for fuelwood in our forest production programme.

An example of the rapidly changing energy scene is provided by Nepal. In a report to the Government of Nepal, Clark (1970) wrote:

The fuelwood shortage promises to become a national catastrophe. Signs of the crisis are obvious throughout Nepal. The desolate eroded hills between the Mahabharat Range and the high Himalayas, the rapidly vanishing vegetation of the hills surrounding the Kathmandu valley, and the constant mud slides along all mountain roads bear grim witness to man's desperate search for fuel and fodder. As the hills are denuded, erosion will increase apace, further destroying the limited farmland and vital roads. The hills will lose even more capacity to support population and increasing numbers of people will be forced into the commercial forests of the Terai. To attempt to protect the water-sheds by administrative action is irrelevant. The only solution is some arrangement to provide the vital commodities, fuel and fodder. To maintain even the present low *per capita* supply of fuelwood, large areas of hill land will have to be reserved for fuel and fodder production. This will accentuate and intensify the land-use problems in the hills, which must already match the land-use problems of the Terai. An afforestation effort of this scope is much too large for His Majesty's Government to handle alone, with the limited resources at their disposal. (Plate 6)

Clark forecast an increasing deficit in meeting the requirements of the Nepalese people because an expanding population demanding more fuel would result in cutting more and more into the forest capital with catastrophe as the end-result if nothing were done to avert it (see Table 5.8).

The result of the incipient fuel shortage can be seen in Nepal in the Terai area bordering India, at Janakpur (see Chapter 7, p. 98), where cow dung is being utilized for fuel as the fuelwood supplies become scarcer. Clark expected *per capita* consumption as well as the total requirement for fuelwood to increase, thus indicating that more would be required for industry than hitherto: he assumed that the

† (103 million m^3, F.A.O. (1972))

TABLE 5.8
Forecast of fuelwood deficit in Nepal

	Forecast requirement	Supply available	Deficit
		million m^3	
1970	2·4	1·5	0·9
1980	3·1	1·5	1·6
1990	4·0	1·5	2·5

Source: Clark (1970)

basic domestic requirements of man at a low income level are relatively inelastic. Clark did not allow for the substitution of electric power in the towns and industries, which are probably the areas where hydro-electric power is likely to satisfy an increasing share of future energy demand in Nepal. In 1970–1 the Government spent over twice as much on the development of electric power as it spent on forestry, but despite this, progress with expansion of hydro-power has been very slow because of the huge capital expenditure required. The economy of Nepal is agrarian, and because of the infrastructural problems, electricity is likely to be only complementary to fuelwood, which must be provided in rural areas if serious social and economic consequences are to be avoided (see Chapter 7).

A further example is taken from Tanzania. Openshaw (1971) used 1960 as a base year in making consumption forecasts for 1980 and 2000: the first, (1980) to provide guidance for short-term industrial development planning and the second (2000) to allow forest policy to be geared to future wood requirements and to provide for long-term industrial and manpower planning. The projections were based upon 1970 consumption of all forest products in Tanzania but because 96 per cent of all wood was used as fuel in 1970, great importance was attached to this aspect of wood usage. Openshaw's methodology for forecasting the future demands for fuelwood included the use of a factor for the degree of urbanization (because of the wide difference between *per capita* cash income in urban and rural areas) in addition to the familiar factors based on growth in population and GNP, see Tables 5.9 to 5.11. He stressed that the forecasts were valid only if the Government policy were to be geared to improving or at least preserving the present wood availability level, and if the country followed a trade policy that sought to maximize returns to the country or the productive factors as a whole and not for the different sectors individually.

Growth of GNP in real terms in Tanzania has been between 5 and 5·25 per cent but the *per capita* GNP increase has been only about 2·5 per cent per annum as a result of a population increase of 2·7 per cent. The Government aims in its five-year plan to increase GNP by 6·7 per cent per annum (a *per capita* increase of 4·0 per cent) by investment in basic industry. The high figures for 1980 and 2000 (Tables 5.9 to 5.11) refer to these aimed increases; the low figures refer to the actual past

Trends affecting fuelwood demand in Tanzania 1970–2000[†]

TABLE 5.9
Population
(millions)

1970	Midyear 1980	2000
13·3	17·4	29·5

Estimated increase 3·1% until 1980, thereafter 2·5%

TABLE 5.10
Urban population
(millions)

1970	Midyear 1980	2000
0·94	1·92	7·05

Estimated increase 9·5% until 1974, thereafter 7%

TABLE 5.11

Gross national product (U.S. $)

	1970	1980 High	1980 Low	2000 High	2000 Low
GNP $ $\times 10^6$	1134	2165	1910	8170	5345
GNP *per capita*	85	125	110	275	180

[†] Source: Openshaw (1971)

growth rate extrapolated into the future. Mean income elasticity of demand for fuelwood was about minus 0·1 i.e. a 20 per cent increase in *per capita* GNP between 1960–70 and a 1·3 per cent decrease in the *per capita* consumption of fuelwood and charcoal.

Three sectors were recognized: rural household, urban household, and non-household/industrial, and the *per capita* consumption in the various sectors was used as the basic unit for forecasting. Substitution of non-wood fuels for fuelwood and charcoal were assumed to be greater at the higher estimate of economic growth (see Table 5.12). Openshaw estimated that fuelwood consumption would double by the year 2000 with charcoal's share of the market increasing from 3 per cent to 25 per cent. Charcoal would be the main fuel by 1980 in urban areas. The use of fuelwood in industry would increase four or five-fold over the same period. Present *per capita* requirements of fuelwood were 2·2 cubic metres per annum but were lower in the capital (1·1 and 1·8 cubic metres) than in the other major centres.

TABLE 5.12

Tanzania—forecast of consumption of fuelwood and charcoal (million m^3)

	Fuelwood					Charcoal[†]				
	1970	1980		2000		1970	1980		2000	
		High	Low	High	Low		High	Low	High	Low
Rural	26·7	30·7	28·4	35·8	29·7	0·3	3·2	1·6	9·9	6·3
Urban	0·8	1·7	1·1	1·4	1·2	0·5	1·1	1·7	4·7	5·6
Industrial	2·1	5·4	4·3	10·7	8·5					
Total	29·6	37·8	33·8	47·9	39·4	0·8	4·3	3·3	14·6	11·9

[†] Roundwood equivalent.   Source: Openshaw (1971)

It was assumed by Openshaw that a decrease in the *per capita* use of forest energy would arise because of the increasing substitution of charcoal (a more ef-ficient fuel) for primary fuel. This assumption is not entirely valid, for the use of charcoal will actually increase the *per capita* consumption of fuelwood. The estimated increase in total fuel consumption will necessitate the establishment of fuelwood plantations on a very large scale unless GNP can be increased much more than expected to meet the enormous extra increase in imported fuels which will otherwise be required.

Studies made in Nepal and Tanzania have shown that actual consumption of fuelwood is far in excess of the amount recorded as being removed from the forest. Official statistics of recorded removals of forest fuel are valuable but consumer surveys are nearly always necessary in order to verify the extent to which official records understate actual consumption. The writer considers that effective planning to serve long-term needs must use forecasts which are based upon reliable estimates of current consumption and analysis of past trends.

Recorded annual removal of fuelwood accounts for almost 50 per cent of the world's total wood removed per annum. Evidence suggests (Table 5.1) that the trend towards the substitution of fossil energy sources for fuelwood in developing economies has reached a plateau and may be declining. The most recently available figures for world fuelwood consumption indicate that demand will decrease in developed countries and increase in developing countries giving an overall rise in the total amount expected to be used. The tendency in developing countries will be to increase the percentage of fuelwood converted to charcoal before use, as urbanization increases the comparative advantage of charcoal over fuelwood for domestic use. In addition economic growth will increase the demand for charcoal for industrial purposes. Developing countries have a comparative advantage over developed countries because of their lower labour rates which will enable them to produce charcoal at lower cost. Provided, therefore, that the necessary skills are developed, there should be new opportunities for increasing exports of charcoal. In developed countries the decline in the consumption of forest energy is likely to slow down if the price of other energy sources continues to increase, and demand for charcoal is likely to increase particularly in specialized fields where secondary forest energy sources are already competitive on technical grounds in their ability to fill a need, for example sulphur-free carbon for refining metals, charcoal for pulverized fuel firing in cement works. In world terms it is suggested that *per capita* consumption of forest energy will be likely to stabilize and eventually increase as cheaper alternative energy supplies become less easily obtainable.

6 The costs and benefits of forest energy supply

'The world is too much with us: Late and soon,
Getting and spending, we lay waste our powers:
Little we see in Nature that is ours;

Wordsworth

The price of forest fuel

If it is assumed that market prices reflect the real worth and utility of commodities to a community, a comparison between the prices of commodities with similar utilities should represent their relative worth and the consequent commercial advantages and disadvantages which might be derived from their use. In countries with undeveloped forest areas and insufficient fossil fuel and other energy resources, forests commonly provide the cheapest energy available in the rural areas. Table 6.1, compiled from average price data for Kenya, Tanzania, and Uganda in 1970, and Table 6.2 for Nepal in 1973, show that fuelwood and charcoal are the cheapest fuels available. A similar study made in India (Uttar Pradesh), Table 6.3, indicates that coal is cheaper than wood and charcoal in industrial areas. A further study made in the United Kingdom, Table 6.4, shows that wood and charcoal are more expensive than most other fuels. Comparison between the price structure of fuel in these countries is made in Table 6.5.

TABLE 6.1

Average market price of fuel and power (U.S. $) *in East Africa in* 1970

Fuel	Retail price	Cost per tonne CE
Wood	7/tonne air dry 20% m.c.	13·80
Charcoal	23/tonne	22·35
Fuel oil	0·21/gallon (43/tonne)	30·28
Paraffin	0·43/gallon (86/tonne)	57·06
Electricity	0·02/unit	134·86
Butane	7/15 kg cylinder	300·00

TABLE 6.2
Average market prices of fuel and power (U.S. $per tonne) in Nepal in 1973

Fuel	Calorific value (CV)	Kathmandu		Terai towns	
		Retail price	Cost per tonne CE	Retail price	Cost per tonne CE
Charcoal	7·1	40	39	30	29
Steam coal	6·3[1]	30–40	38	31–36	36·7
Wood	3·5	24	47	22	43
Paraffin	10·4	112	74		74
Electricity		0·01/unit industrial rate	80	0·05/unit	401
		0·075/unit domestic rate	600		not applicable

TABLE 6.3
Average market prices of fuel and power (U.S. $ per tonne) in India in 1973

Fuel	CV	Wholesale price	Lucknow and Kanpur Retail price	Cost tonne CE
Soft coke	6·9[2]	23	28	28
Steam coal	6·3[1]	23	28	31
Wood	3·5	8–15	22	43
Hard coke	7·1[2]	38	46	45
Charcoal	7·1	30–45	33–69	49
Paraffin	10·4		96	64
Electricity			0·05/unit	401

[1] Calorific value has been reduced for this coal as it contains 20% ash.

[2] Calorific value has been estimated.

The tables show that forest fuels provide the cheapest source of energy in developing countries unless indigenous fossil fuels are available. What is not explained is why many developing countries with ample forests to provide for their domestic household needs prefer to import coal and oil for industrial use. The reason for this anomaly is that the necessary entrepreneurship, infrastructure, and technology for converting wood to fuels such as charcoal (solid), methyl alcohol (liquid), or carbon monoxide and hydrogen (gas) have not been developed to make the use of forest energy competitive in a world economy geared to the use of erstwhile cheap and somewhat more convenient fossil fuels. Wood also is cheap when 'mined' but because it tends to be dispersed, the gathering operations do not lend themselves so readily to economies of scale as does the exploitation of concentrated resources.

TABLE 6.4

*Average market prices of fuel and power (U.S. $) in the
United Kingdom in July 1973*

Fuel	CV	Retail price	Cost tonne CE
Coal industrial	6·9	23·75/tonne	24
Fuel oil[†]	10·1	0·23/gallon (52·50/tonne)	36
Paraffin	10·4	0·3–0·4/gall. (60–85/tonne)	40–56
Wood	3·5	25/tonne	49
Charcoal	7·1	175/tonne	170
Electricity domestic		0·025/unit	200
Butane	10·8	580/tonne	370

† Oil prices have been subject to sharp increases since this table was compiled.

TABLE 6.5

*Relative costs of fuels and power compared on the same calorific value basis in
five different areas (Fuelwood taken as unity)*

Fuel	E. Africa (1970)	India (1973)	Nepal (1973) Kathmandu	Terai towns	U.K. (1973)
Fuelwood	1·0	1·0	1·0	1·0	1·0
Charcoal	1·6	1·1	0·8	0·7	3·5
Coal	–	0·7	0·8	0·9	0·5
Fuel oil	2·0	–	–	–	0·7
Paraffin	4·0	1·5	1·6	1·6	0·7–1·0
Electricity	8·9	9·3	8·5 (domestic)	9·3	4·1
Butane	19·8	–	–	–	15·4

N.B. The costs of a particular fuel are not comparable between areas

A measure of the underpricing of wood can be made by an analysis of the costs of growing forest produce on bare land. These are costs which are not borne by exploitation of natural forest unless the royalty payments are large enough to cover the costs of ensuring the growth of a replacement crop.

Fuelwood

The main items affecting the ultimate price of fuelwood are the value of the raw material (growing costs), and payments for cutting and preparation, transport and storage.

The value of the raw material. The costs of preparing and transporting fuelwood are comparatively high and therefore the possibility of making savings in expenditure on growing the raw material should always be examined. Two examples illustrating the benefits obtainable from marginal opportunities are taken from Uganda: the reduction in the costs of silvicultural operations by the utilization of forest waste; and the reduction of the establishment costs of fuel plantations by *taungya* cultivation.

In Uganda the main objective of management for the forest reserves is to grow quality timber, but because many of the trees in the forests are not in the 'quality' category they were formerly poisoned in order to afford more room for the valuable timber-producing species. In this situation it is obviously advantageous for the Forest Department to have the 'undesirable' trees removed without the expense of purchasing arboricides. A system (the Mengo system) was worked out whereby fuelwood-cutters and charcoal-makers are issued with licences to cut and remove the trees selected by the Forest Department (Earl 1968). The 'cost of growing' the fuelwood is therefore only marginal to the cost of protecting and managing the forest, plus the small amount of extra cash involved in selecting and marketing the trees and checking the removal operation. The return to the Government per unit of stacked wood cut more than covers operating costs (although the royalty, equivalent to 0·1 man/days per stère, is less than that charged for wood sold in plantations). If the savings on arboricides are counted as benefits, the system is not only cost-effective but makes very considerable returns to the nation. This silvicultural method could be adopted with advantage elsewhere where it is possible to obtain good managerial control.

In other parts of Uganda, because of the lack of indigenous forest, fuel plantations have been established (Plate 7). The production cost of fuelwood from Eucalyptus plantations on a medium site (index 30) (Kingston 1972) is U.S. $4 per tonne CE and less than U.S. $2 per tonne CE if *taungya* is practised. (See Appendix 2).

Payments for cutting and preparation. In most countries the forests are controlled by the state, which has responsibility for ensuring that all produce removed is properly licenced and recorded. Although this control of timber concessions is usually well organized, the preparation and sale of fuelwood and charcoal is quite often indiscriminate and insufficiently well supervised. Studies made under controlled conditions have established that over a wide range of conditions in the tropics an average of 2 stères is a reasonable daily output if trees are felled and cut into 0·5-metre lengths using hand tools, i.e. 0·5 man-days per stère equivalent to U.S. $0·36 in Uganda (Earl 1973a).

Transport. The cost of transport is the most critical factor determining whether fuelwood will be marketable at a price competitive with other fuels. As carriage is usually charged by weight and not volume, it is essential to reduce the moisture content of fuelwood in order to lower the costs of the transport in terms of CE per tonne/kilometre.

Storage. Unless fuelwood is well dried out, its comparatively low calorific value may lead to abnormally high storage costs. Wood which is cut and then left to dry incurs interest charges on the costs of cutting and preparation and therefore the 'benefits' of having dry wood have to be weighed against the 'costs' of waiting for the returns on the expenditure involved in wood preparation. If theft is rare, the stacks may be left in the forest for a few weeks in order to take advantage of the initial rapid loss of weight which occurs and also to delay the payment of transport charges. Later the wood may be moved for final drying-out under open conditions nearer to the place of consumption.

Charcoal

Charcoal is most profitable when produced from low-cost material, for example, natural forest thinnings or sawmill waste, but is much less so when the cost of growing trees has to be taken into account. Apart from the manufacturing cost, the main reason for this is that the conversion rate wood : charcoal, in kilns is approximately 4 : 1, which increases the raw material costs by the same ratio, thus improving the comparative advantage of fuelwood over charcoal.

In order to produce charcoal for sale at the forest site at U.S. $24 per tonne, including profits and overheads, (see Table 6.6) the charcoal operations would have to be subsidized if trees were grown for the purpose unless *taungya* were used during plantation establishment. The largest profit would be obtained if wood were available from the results of silvicultural operations in the natural forest.

TABLE 6.6

Cost per tonne of production of charcoal in U.S. $ including profits and overheads

Country	Cost of production per tonne	Remarks	Source
Uganda	20·00	Lambiotte retort depreciated over 30 years no profit element included	Aldred (personal communication)
Uganda	24·00	Portable kilns	Earl (1970)
Madagascar	23·60	Portable kilns	Earl (1971)
Ivory Coast	23·20	Portable kilns	Earl (1972a)
Nepal	19·00	Portable kilns	Earl (1973b)
U.S.A.	40·00–98·00	All installation types, costs updated to 1971	U.S.D.A. (1961)

Choice of carbonization technique. The choice of the best method of carbonization must depend heavily upon the location and costs of transporting the raw material. Fixed installations are ideal for undertakings which have available sufficient continuous supplies of low-cost raw materials which can be usefully up-graded to charcoal on the site. Suitable locations for fixed kilns or retorts are near primary industries such as sawmills and occasionally at secondary industries such as match factories, furniture factories, and tanning works. Most wood available for charcoal manufacture, however, is not concentrated at depots and is usually widely dispersed within forests in the more remote areas. It is in these situations that portable kilns can best be utilized to reduce the cost of accumulation and transport of raw materials. This comparative advantage enjoyed by some countries in having cheap labour gives support to the economic argument for using portable kilns which are generally cheaper and more labour-intensive than other types of kilns, with the exception of the traditional earth kilns, and do not necessarily require inputs of capital for wood-moving equipment. Figures taken from Earl and Mabonga-Mwisaka (1969) indicate that it would be cheaper to use portable rather than fixed kilns in Uganda, but for the U.S.A. the reverse would be true because of the vastly greater cost of labour.

The costs of production of charcoal depend upon the price paid for raw material as well as the labour costs and method of carbonization, but for a number of African countries it is remarkably constant.

Charcoal produced by traditional earth kilns is extremely difficult to cost because of the great variation in yields, but in Uganda (where on average a man used 15·4 stères of wood per month to make about a tonne of charcoal) the labour costs, if given a market value, were in 1971 about U.S. $20 per tonne.

Transport economics—fuelwood and charcoal

In rural areas fuelwood is usually cheaper than charcoal for heating and cooking purposes, but even in well-wooded regions it is not always possible to sustain the supply of fuelwood to industrialists and urban dwellers because the forests closest to the areas of consumption are usually those most likely to be converted to other uses. Charcoal has an increasing comparative price advantage over fuelwood as development progresses and the source of production becomes further removed from consumption centres because of its higher calorific value and special chemical properties. Although charcoal has a higher thermal capacity per unit weight than wood, the conversion loss involved in carbonization and the manufacturing costs usually set a lower economic limit to the distance which can be covered when it is to be used solely for heating purposes. The limiting lower and upper economic distance constraints which may be applicable to any country will be affected by the prices charged for alternative fuels, as well as the freight charges; for example, India has an efficient railway system and low rates whereas Nepal has virtually no railways and has expensive road haulage services.

It takes approximately 4 tonnes of dry wood to provide 1 tonne of charcoal, and 1 tonne of charcoal contains about twice the calorific value of the same weight of dry wood: consequently it is better to burn wood where transport costs are negligible, provided that the wood can be dried to about 30 per cent moisture content and there is not too much concern about the smoke. However, once transport costs become significant, because they are twice as much per calorie for wood as for charcoal, the point is soon reached when it becomes preferable to use charcoal. To find the haulage distances at which charcoal manufacture for normal heating purposes becomes worth while it is necessary to know the costs of production, the distance between forest and market, and the costs per tonne/kilometre. Fig. 6.1 has been drawn using basic cost data appertaining to East Africa in 1970.

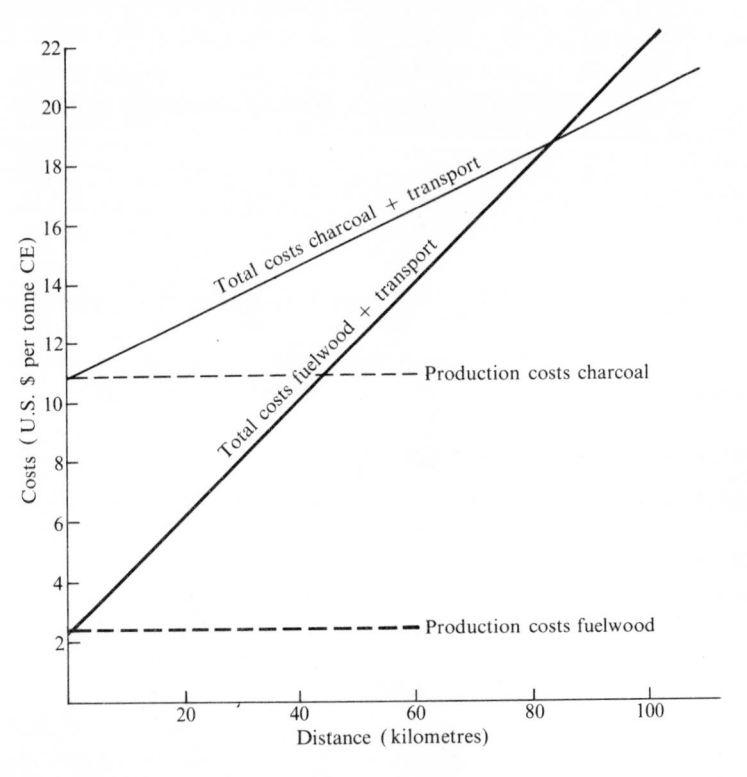

Fig. 6.1. Net production costs (U.S. $) per tonne CE of fuelwood and charcoal from natural forest, East Africa (1970). Based on Table 6.7 (p. 75).

The point of indifference between the cost of producing and transporting fuelwood or charcoal on an equivalent thermal content basis is 82 kilometres, i.e. at distances less than 82 kilometres the marginal value of heat from fuelwood is higher than that obtainable from charcoal and at distances greater than 82 kilometres the position is reversed. Consumer preference is a governing factor in determining the final market price, since qualities other than heating ability (e.g. smokelessness) play a part. In Uganda, charcoal completely dominates the domestic fuel market in towns, whereas in Kathmandu, Nepal, wood is preferred and charcoal is relatively unimportant.

TABLE 6.7

Production and transport costs, U.S. $, per tonne of fuelwood and charcoal (excluding overheads and profit) in East Africa in 1970. (Wage rate U.S. $0·72 per man/day)

	Plantation without *taungya*	Plantation with *taungya*	Natural forest	Plantation without *taungya*	Plantation with *taungya*	Natural forest
	Fuelwood			Charcoal		
Royalty/net cost of raw material	2·38	1·08	0·14	9·52	4·32	0·56
Conversion costs	1·08	1·08	1·08	10·18[†]	10·18[†]	10·18[†]
Total costs at site[‡]	3·46	2·16	1·22	19·70	14·50	10·74
Costs including transport 35 km	6·96	5·66	4·72	23·20	18·00	14·24
Costs including transport 70 km	10·46	9·16	8·22	26·70	21·50	17·74
Costs including transport 100 km	13·46	12·16	11·22	29·70	24·50	20·74

Transport costs U.S. $0·10 per tonne/km. [†] Earl (1973a). [‡] Assumes 3 stères per tonne at 30 per cent moisture content

Financial analysis

Profitability represents a useful yardstick for measuring the efficiency of a business enterprise from the owner's point of view but it does not necessarily measure the value of the activity to the community as a whole. The market economy does not reflect the true costs of the individual enterprises of which it is comprised because many activities affecting the public interest are not priced through the market and perfect competition in all economic activities does not prevail. Likewise the true benefits to society of many social goods are not adequately represented by prices. This appears to be true of forest fuel in those societies where it has for long been regarded as a free social good. The unrestricted market system is particularly unsuitable for dealing with situations in which the objective function of development is not only maximization of production, compatible with satisfaction of demand, but includes concern for the long-term effects upon welfare and resources. This analysis of the situation is not intended to condemn private entrepreneurial skill, which in many countries plays an essential part in the production and distribution process, the objective is to point out that because the interests of private enterprise are necessarily vested, a certain amount of control needs to be exercised in order to reconcile the activities of the entrepreneurs with the needs of society as a whole.

Strategic policies for scarce resources should be made by governments after taking into account all the advantages and disadvantages of various possible courses of action and their effect upon the people in the long-term as well as the short-term. The production, distribution, and marketing of the goods and services can be left to private or public enterprise, or a mixture of the two as desired, provided that sufficient care has been taken to ensure that net long-term benefit to the nation is not jeopardized by short-term profit motivation.

Economic analysis

Economic analysis attempts to determine the holistic return to the whole society or economy from all the resources committed to a project regardless of who in society contributes them and regardless of who in the society receives the benefits. This is the social or economic return. Economic analyses are equally valid in helping to choose the most remunerative alternative from the social standpoint, whether the capital is to come from public revenues or from private sources, whether there are income taxes or not, or whether the project is to be in the public sector or is to be operated by individuals on their own behalf. The three most important aspects which distinguish economic analysis from financial analysis are: shadow or accounting prices may be used to reflect better true social or economic values; taxes and subsidies are treated as transfer payments (taxes are benefits to society as a whole and subsidies are costs); interest on capital is not deducted from total returns since it is part of the total return to capital available to society.

Cost–benefit analysis

Cost–benefit analysis is a specialized type of economic analysis in which values are attached to all goods and services whether or not they are priced through the market, and the 'true' discounted costs and discounted benefits expected to arise from a project are compared at a common point in time and expressed as a simple ratio. Because cost–benefit analysis attempts to quantify and bring into the analysis all the long-term effects of a course of action upon land and resources, its use could and should be extended to decisions involving the apportionment of land for fuel production in developing countries.

Social cost–benefit analysis needs to be used by some aid agencies in the appraisal of schemes which might qualify for their aid. Little and Mirrlees (1969) have written a manual for the Organization for Economic Co-operation and Development in which it is suggested that shadow prices based upon world prices should be used for all resources needed in a project. Despite the difficulties inherent in this requirement, the British and German aid agencies have brought out their own manuals based on the Little–Mirrlees principle. It is often difficult to assess the 'true value' of non-marketable products with precision, and the method has many critics mainly for this reason. The analysis is nevertheless likely to lead to increasingly better decision-making as its use is extended to policy problems.

Assuming that the central planning department of a country has encouraged its forest authorities to provide fuel from forests and plantations for the domestic and industrial needs of the nation, the individual entrepreneur or aid agency should be able to make feasibility studies of individual project proposals to supply fuelwood or charcoal to the various markets. Financial appraisals using discounted cash flow techniques are normally sufficient to establish whether or not an individual project is viable but economic analysis is usually needed to ensure that the net social benefit is positive whenever government participation or international aid is required.

The sum total of all costs and benefits from viable enterprises, which may in some cases need to be encouraged by fiscal and other measures, should fit into the plan for the provision of fuel for the country as a whole. A full description of the measures needed to promote a profitable charcoal industry in a country is given by Earl (1973a). The active participation of the forest authority in the promotion of a viable forest fuel enterprise for a country is a necessary prerequisite for the success of projects which aim to meet the real needs of the people. Often the social benefits of forestry have been largely ignored by foresters (Earl 1972b).

Economic and social benefits from forest energy

It has been shown that in developing countries with abundant forests, the cheapest and most practical supplies of energy are often provided by fuelwood and charcoal: in most developed economies and in those developing countries with inadequate forest cover, other sources often provide energy more cheaply than does forest fuel. There is no reason, however, to assume that because a fuel is cheaper in some countries and dearer in others that the net economic benefit obtained by its use in either developing or developed economies is necessarily related to its market price. In some regions of developing countries where low income and meagre fuel supplies prevail, the financial returns to forest authorities from investment in fuelwood plantations may not exceed the marginal investment rate but the social benefits are often very high. One reason for the low rate of return is that the social cost of labour, in conditions of under-employment is sometimes very much lower than the wages that a forest authority has to pay. The cost of growing fuelwood may thus bear an indirect tax paid as a subsidy to the labour force.

A policy decision that the use of fuelwood and charcoal should be discouraged because imported fuel will be cheaper should be made only after a thorough examination of all the possible social benefits and disbenefits which might arise from a proposed change in customary energy-use; this can be made only by the use of the technique of cost—benefit analysis. It cannot be denied that in many countries fossil fuels are cheaper to use than forest energy but the comparative advantage that some developing countries have over developed countries in the cost of production of forest fuel will be enhanced in an economic analysis if all the social costs and benefits involved are taken in account; e.g. shadow pricing of labour will often reduce the true cost of producing forest fuel to below the market cost.

The economic benefits which may be derived from the active encouragement of the extension of the use of forest energy sources can be divided into direct, indirect, and intangible.

Direct benefits. The most obvious manifestation of a direct benefit is the profit obtainable from a marketable product with a value which can be measured by the consumers' willingness to pay. The money return to the country may be a result of direct participation by the state in the enterprise or from taxation or royalties, but there should always be an increase in national wealth in real terms. Distribution is often left to private enterprise; provided that there are enough trained people available, business firms working to a profit motive can be more efficient than state-run enterprises. In developing countries it is often a shortage of entrepreneurial skill which inhibits the development of more efficient means of production and marketing of goods (charcoal for example). The help of the government or an aid agency in providing necessary training is often invaluable in the early stages of a new project. Because of the long-term planning required and the high capital needs of forest projects, it is usually necessary for the state to organize, manage, and grow the trees in the manner, time, and place required in order that entrepreneurs can purchase the raw material for conversion and sale. Large firms requiring massive supplies of fuelwood and charcoal, e.g. tobacco companies, cement industries, and steelworks, sometimes manage to grow their own wood supplies but usually this is done in close collaboration with the forest authority.

From the point of view of forest economics, the most important benefit is the effect which fuelwood utilization and charcoal manufacture have on increasing the total profitability of the forests. The species composition of tropical forests is such that poisoning or other form of removal of competititive vegetation has sometimes to be carried out in order to enhance the growth of the desired future crop. In many situations the general demand for energy can be converted into an effective demand for fuelwood and charcoal by good public relations work, thereby creating a market for hitherto unsaleable produce. Although it is not usual to credit the revenue derived from a fuelwood or charcoal refining operation to offset the costs of treatment of the future crop of timber, it is useful to point out that money saved, which would otherwise have been spent on arboricide or unremunerative cultural operations, vastly increases the net worth of forests when discounted cash flow techniques are used for appraisal of the value of the forest enterprise.

Indirect benefits. Work provided for men who were previously unemployed and transfer of labour from subsistence farming to creative work are net benefits to society as a whole, not only because of the extra production obtained from the provision of employment but also because of the possibility of collecting taxes for government projects which will in turn generate more employment. Forest fuel production is labour-intensive and shares with many other operations in forestry the distinction of maximizing employment together with maximizing output. There can be conflicts in some industrial production techniques where, for example, the capital : output ratio for a modern-style textile industry may be lower than that for a primitive, more labour-intensive system (Stewart and Streeten 1973). Although there is little conflict between the output and employment objectives in developing countries over forest fuel production, conflict can occur in charcoal manufacture. An industry based on traditional earth kilns has an infinitesimally small capital:output ratio, whereas one based on simple portable steel kilns requiring only modest investment inputs necessarily has a larger capital:output ratio but increases production per man and per unit input of raw material by a factor of 3. Fortunately many charcoal-making industries are operating under conditions of increasing demand for charcoal in preference to wood, and men are easily persuaded to convert fuelwood into charcoal when they appreciate the advantage that the added value makes to their profits. The conversion of fuelwood into charcoal may be a labour-intensive, low-investment opportunity which has a direct appeal for those countries making the transition from a subsistence to a monied economy. All the rudimentary skills of business management can be learnt by apprentices in a charcoal industry, an industry which has potential for obtaining still further added value by the establishment of briquetting and activation processes.

As money obtained from sales of fuelwood and charcoal in the towns is paid to workers in the country, extra labour employed in the rural sector has a useful horizontal distributive effect upon national income which is usually weighed unfairly in favour of the urban worker. There are signs that urbanization is occurring too rapidly in many developing countries with consequential problems of increase in crime and other undesirable anti-social trends which can be partly reduced by providing incentives for people to remain in the rural areas.

Employment in the forest rural sector improves the vertical distribution of money since there is a smaller income differential between the upper and lower echelons in a forest fuel business than in industries which have to rely upon a top level cadre of expatriates or scarce, qualified local staff.

Financial analysis does not show benefits from saving in foreign exchange although in cost—benefit analysis the usual procedure is to establish shadow prices for the foreign exchange derived from opportunity costs (in terms of other imports foregone) and to set these against the calculated opportunity costs of capital at home. For some countries this saving is potential, because the available increment of forest fuel is enough to meet the population's energy requirements. In most developing countries, however, the use of forest fuel for domestic cooking and heating generally represents an unappreciated saving in fuel imports. If these savings could be extended to the growing industrial sector, the total benefits would far exceed those that are immediately obvious. The destruction of forests without making sufficient allowance for future needs and the inability of many countries to stem exponential population growth makes the need for a re-appraisal of the role of forests in providing for the energy needs of development one of the utmost urgency. In those countries without the means of creating surplus foreign exchange to buy imported fuel, the loss of forest energy wealth is likely to be particularly serious for succeeding generations.

It seldom pays to export fuelwood because of its very low value-to-bulk ratio. If enough capital and technical skill are available, fuelwood may be converted to products of the right quality and quantity so as to provide an extremely valuable export outlet to those developed countries that are deficient in forests and require charcoal for both industrial and domestic use. It must be remembered that ex- porting is an expensive business because of the extra costs of carriage and market- ing. Briquetted charcoal, activated charcoal, and the by-products of distillation therefore stand a better chance than lump charcoal of providing useful exports because the value added in the conversion process drastically increases the value-to-bulk ratio.

Most industries produce 'linkage effects' but not all of them can claim to be able to diffuse these benefits into the rural communities. The improvement of charcoal-making techniques might well stimulate local firms to manufacture kilns (backward linkage) and the provision of reliable supplies of fuelwood might en- courage factories to expand by using local fuel (forward linkage). The provision of a fuel base for industry is probably a major factor in the decision-making process, which has to determine whether or not industrialization in a particular sphere is feasible. In Uganda, the national deposits of iron ore might have been exported if it had not been pointed out that charcoal from the forests could provide the necessary chemical for reducing the iron ore as efficiently as imported coke or gas. The techniques used in smelting iron ore with charcoal are extremely old but nevertheless are of the type that offer the most practical solution to the problems facing developing countries who wish to attain economic independence.

Charcoal is smokeless fuel which when used domestically provides a sol- ution to the pollution problems of some of the larger cities in the tropics. The beneficial effects of using charcoal in preference to smoky fuels in cities are not at present appreciated fully in developing countries but this factor could be important at a later stage of development, e.g. if clean air legislation were intro- duced as in the United Kingdom.

Intangible benefits. These are more difficult to define since they are subjective and vague. The encouragement of self-reliance, conservation of the world's fossil fuel resources, war on waste, creation of a dynamic rural environment, amenity, and recreation can all be considered as healthy spillovers from the operation of providing renewable fuel from forests, whether they are natural forests (made productive enough to justify their retention) or plantations created especially for fuel.

Economic costs of forest energy

The economic costs of forest fuel production, as in other activities, are mainly based upon the concept of opportunity cost. The opportunity cost of producing fuelwood and charcoal is equivalent to the 'net input', which may be defined as the goods and services withdrawn from the rest of the economy that would have been used elsewhere if fuelwood and charcoal had not been produced. The main physical inputs for forest fuel production are land, labour, capital and the wood itself.

The opportunity cost of land is equal to the loss of potential output from the land because of its use for growing trees. This value depends very much upon the degree of population pressure for the land, the agricultural potential of the soil, and the weighting given to the indirect benefits from having forests. If the forests are there because a conglomerate of benefits has been judged to justify their retention and there is a policy constraint upon using the land for any other purpose, it is fruitless to analyse the possible effects of such a change taking place. If the forests are not extensive enough to provide fuel for the population, the analysis of costs must take into account the opportunity costs of growing trees on the sites available for afforestation. This is commonly very low because subsistence agriculture provides for most of the basic needs of the people and any national analysis of the opportunity cost of land used for fuel plantations would therefore need to allow for the possibility that agricultural land might be used more efficiently. An overriding consideration might be that the lack of forest fuel in an area could drive the people to use cow dung for fuel, which could have an adverse effect on the soil. Here the forest authority could be empowered to plant selected areas throughout the community to fulfil a social need for fuel and at the same time help to conserve long-term soil fertility. Fuelwood and charcoal production will result in fuller utilization of available nutrients. The loss of these nutrients might lead to loss of productivity, particularly on sites where soils are base-deficient. The possibility of returning ash or the addition of limestone should be considered and the value and costs of those additions needed to maintain fertility should be taken into account.

The opportunity cost of labour is equal to the productive capacity foregone by taking up employment on fuel production. In many developing countries the cost of any work created amounts to no more than the goods which the labourer produces himself on his holding, and since this is usually made up by other members of his family the cost amounts to zero because there is no effective alternative employment. In such a situation a surrogate (shadow) wage rate should be used in order to value properly the extent of the cost of the change in employment of labour.

The effective opportunity cost of wood that may be used for fuelwood or charcoal (e.g. wood residues and secondary species) is usually nil or very low because it is generally of such poor quality as to be unsuitable for conversion to other use. The potential opportunity cost of wood used for fuel or charcoal must, however, be borne in mind because of the possibility of fabricating pulp, paper, hard and soft boards from particles of inferior base material. Most conversion processes require inputs of energy themselves and it is therefore necessary to look very carefully at all the energy inputs and outputs required in the manufacture of new products before assuming that a particle-board industry would maximize the returns available from the utilization of poor quality wood. Obviously the economic and social returns from board-mills, even in conditions of fuel scarcity, may be high enough to justify utilizing material suitable for fuelwood and charcoal and importing fuel for the nation's energy needs, but for countries without fossil fuels it could be more advantageous to grow timber and fuel enough to meet home demand. Provided that there is enough wood available, the ideal solution may be a compromise, with wood being apportioned its place according to the social and economic advantages as well as to purely financial criteria.

The opportunity cost of capital is the return foregone on the capital invested in the production of forest energy. Usually this is taken at the marginal investment rate. The rate is used in calculations for determining the profitability of projects in discounted cash flow analysis and as the 'cut off' rate in ranking projects by the use of the internal rate of return criterion.

The social and institutional constraints affecting the utilization of forest energy

Outside towns in much of the tropical developing world, fuelwood is often regarded as a free good and even when forests are placed under management most forest services make special concessions for villagers to remove dead trees and branches for their own use free of charge, or at nominal fee. Many others provide facilities for local people to hew and remove wood at preferential rates. For example, the Nepal Forest Service charges local people only U.S. \$0·15 for a bullock cart-load of wood but commercial firms and townspeople are charged U.S. \$0·5. This tendency for fuelwood to be regarded as a social good also has origins in the developed countries; for example, persons residing within certain of the ancient royal forests in England are provided with free cords of wood every year. It is the assumption of the right to free fuel or the granting of privileges to persons to have fuelwood, free or at reduced prices, which has led to an undervaluation of the true worth of forest fuel in many countries. There is also a move by some advisers from 'developed' countries to convert people away from the use of forest energy sources, either from the conviction that this will stem the destruction of trees or from a desire to 'modernize' the economy. There is a widely held belief that the use of fuelwood or charcoal for the production of energy is primitive and that the conversion to gas, coal, oil, or electricity is indicative of social and economic progress. Examples are sometimes given of the correlation between high GNP and low fuelwood consumption in developed countries such as France, the United Kingdom, and the United States as if to prove the case.

Kernan (1968) is a report for Vietnam states that:

In an economically mature society such as that of the United States, wood for burning accounts for seven per cent of all timber used and generates two per cent of all the energy produced from energy materials. This trend is necessary, irreversible and on the whole beneficial. In Vietnam neither fuelwood nor charcoal represents an economic opportunity closely allied to the most dynamic and forward looking sectors of the economy. Under these circumstances the Forestry Administration need not be overly concerned about the long-term supply of fuelwood and charcoal wood, about restricting their cutting, or least of all, about collecting small sums of money for their removal from the public domain.

Apart from asking how the people are to purchase such vast quantities of alternative fuel and where is it to come from, we need to ask why it is necessarily economically and socially unsound to use charcoal in preference to imported fuels. The chief reason why fuelwood and charcoal are not used as much as formerly in the developed countries is that they have become scarcer and more expensive than alternative fuels. Convenience is sometimes cited as a reason for the change, but this is not a valid argument, for there is nothing particularly difficult in the use of charcoal which cannot be overcome by technology as was done for gas, oil, and coal. In many of the developed economies it is now only richer people who can afford to maintain an open wood fire in the living room or a charcoal grill in the garden. As has been shown earlier in this chapter, there are situations in which indigenous fuelwood or charcoal are cheaper and more efficient than imported fossil fuels and have the added advantages of making a contribution to the balance of payments and of generating important social benefits for the people in the country concerned.

In Asia the problem of development is seen by Nowak and Polycarpou (1969) as one of energy shortage and this is a danger to agriculture (because of dung being burnt).

Future development of Asian economy will depend to a large extent on the availability of suitable sources of energy.

Lack of mineral fuels (or electric energy) in rural societies initiates a chain reaction which not only has adverse repercussions on the forestry sector but on the whole economy. Demands for firewood are in excess of supply and animal dung is extensively used to supplement fuelwood. This deprives agriculture of valuable organic fertilizer, hence crop yields are low and low crop returns per unit of land cannot feed a rapidly growing population. From this stems the problem of land hunger; more land is brought under the plough to produce more food, leaving no room for fuelwood plantations.

Development and the forest energy resource

The situation in developing countries today is in some important respects quite different from that which prevailed in the now advanced countries when the exploitation of forest fuel was the main or only source of energy.

Leslie (1971) suggests that there are reasons for believing that exploitation of the tropical forests in developing countries is not likely to repeat, on anything like the same scale, the propulsive effect that forest exploitation had in the emerging countries of the fairly recent past. On the contrary, it could be held that the exploitation, which gave an impetus to development in now advanced countries, has led to the export to the developing countries of institutions, attitudes, and materials which now tend to act as a brake on the development potential of such resources as forests. The importance of forestry for accelerating economic development has been pointed out by Westoby (1963), who emphasized the importance of linkage effects. Forest industries have a relatively high demand for labour and locally produced or existing raw materials and have well-developed multiplier effects, external economies, foreign exchange earnings, and import-replacement capacities which can combine to make significant contributions of the kind generally considered to be needed for economic development. Although Westoby was thinking of forestry and forest industry in general, his deductions can be applied with equal force to the forest-fuel sector of forestry.

Land-settlement schemes are recognized as providing opportunities for governments to effect social reform. The *Provisional indicative world plan for agricultural development* (F.A.O. 1970b) gives the F.A.O. view on the place of land settlement in overall development but makes no mention of the necessity of providing for the future fuel needs of the settlers. Formerly, land-settlement meant that families moved into the forest and cleared land in order to farm, or that land was made available to settlers after government agencies has completed large irrigation projects or land-reclamation schemes. Only recently have settlement schemes come to be considered as devices which can be used to repair the weaknesses in the existing agrarian structures. In attempting to introduce an integrated approach, some countries have either failed to achieve the integration desired by creating farming communities which are not socially or economically viable or have built integrated schemes which are too expensive for settlers to afford. The future need in all regions is for the design and implementation of land-settlement projects that farmers can afford and which achieve integration within the agrarian structure. There is a great need for settlement projects that will not require outlays of capital until the new communities can afford to bear them. This requires careful and restrained planning.

Planning settlement schemes appears to offer a great opportunity to reverse the trend of ignoring the social and economic benefits available from renewable energy from forests.

The development of an indigenous forest fuel industry cannot be considered independently of its viability in terms of world market prices. Although it may be economically advantageous, up to a certain point, to produce something rather than import it, there is no particular economic advantage in self-sufficiency in itself, particularly if it is obtained at a high opportunity cost in terms of scarce, skilled labour and capital resources. The development advantage of forest industries, or of any other industry for that matter, would soon disappear if there were no comparative advantage after taking into account all relevant social costs and benefits. The chief difficulty in establishing a quantitative basis for assessing the contribution which the forest fuel industry makes to development is confounded by the fact that the products of the industry tend to be dispersed and accepted as social goods. Charcoal industries have recently been developed in many countries which are making a small but significant contribution to the economies of those countries. There is considerable advantage in encouraging the development of small industries. Sutton (1973) has shown that some of the most efficient sawmills are those run as family concerns and economies of scale reputed to be obtainable from large, integrated sawmills do not always apply. In developing countries small industries (of which a charcoal industry would be a typical example) should be encouraged for the following reasons.

(1) Small industries help to economize scarce capital for employment; their capital/labour ratio is low, since a unit of capital invested in a small undertaking generally creates more employment than a unit invested in a heavily mechanized, large-scale industry.
(2) The small entrepreneurs are often able to pool local funds obtained from their families and friends, and thus capital becomes available for productive purposes which would otherwise not be utilized.
(3) Small enterprises require fewer managerial and supervisory skills and can take advantage of traditional abilities.
(4) Small industries help to preserve a balance between the rate of economic growth in urban and rural areas.

It is easy to see the possible advantages which may accrue from the establishment of small rural industries from examination of the rate of growth of the charcoal industry in Uganda over 10 years from 1963–71 (see Table 6.8). The benefits to the economy of 3890 men, each earning perhaps U.S. $300 per annum more than they would have done before, are obvious but not easily detectable in national

TABLE 6.8
Charcoal consumption trend–Uganda ·

Year	Home produced tonnes	Number of men on production[†]	Imported tonnes
1962–3	200	15	22 000
1963–4	700	49	25 000
1964–5	1200	84	27 000
1965–6	3024	140	29 000
1966–7	6000	270	29 500
1967–8	10 000	550	30 000
1968–9	21 500	1400	30 000
1969–70	48 820	3200	21 000
1970–1	58 535	3660	17 000
1971–2	63 656	3890	17 000

Source: Annual report of the Uganda Forest Department   [†] Estimated.

accounts. It is therefore difficult to assess quantitatively whether or not any particular sector of the economy makes a significant contribution to development unless calculations are made in a piecemeal fashion for individual sub-sectors.

The forest energy opportunity

The direct and indirect benefits derivable from utilization of the forest fuel resource have been discussed in this chapter but the critical factor of relevance to the theme of this book is whether the capacity of forest fuel to assist in economic and social development is relatively greater or less than feasible alternative uses of the forest and land resources. Forests can be managed so as to make a contribution to economic development by the provision of fuel along with timber; but in order for the full potential of this opportunity to be realizeable, the forest and economic policies must develop on the basis of meeting the real needs of the people concurrent with the establishment of vertically integrated domestic industries. On such a basis, the prospect of a world shortage of energy resources offers an opportunity for those countries with ample forests to take up the chance to develop the comparative advantage at present enjoyed chiefly by those with plentiful fossil-fuel resources.

7 Planning the forest energy supply

'It's not as easy as it looks;
It'll take longer than you think:
It'll cost more than you've budgeted for:
If anything can go wrong it will.'

Attributed to Murphy (Irish King 6th century AD)

The substitution of alternative energy supplies for forest fuel in developing economies is by no means certain, and in many countries the substitution process is not socially justifiable. Developed countries with adequate forests could also, with advantage, provide more energy from their indigenous renewable resources as a contingency against possible interruptions in the supply of fuel and power from fossil sources.

Fuelwood and charcoal can make the most immediate economic and social contribution to development in regions that have incompletely utilized forests and whose indigenous energy resources are otherwise inadequate. As forests can sustain fuelwood supplies only if their provision is made a conscious aim of management, it is essential for a country to have an active forest energy policy. This policy should be formulated only after analysis of all the relevant social and economic factors. Any plan for energy from forests should be in accord with the long-term planning objectives of the country concerned, because land utilized for growing trees would not generally be available for other productive purposes. The production of forest energy would commonly have only a small opportunity cost, for existing reserved timber production forests could be managed so as to provide fuelwood and charcoal as 'benefits' additional to those already enjoyed. The management of this energy supply must be well planned if needless liquidation of much of the existing forest capital is to be avoided. Plans must have clearly defined objectives and must make due allowance for risk and uncertainty if they are to succeed.

Planning at the national and sectoral level

This will seek to cover most of the following ground: clarification of objectives; evaluation of present and forecast of future demand both effective and potential; an assessment of available resources; assessment of ways of meeting the objectives; selection of suitable projects; and establishment of priorities. The planning will suggest how implementation should be carried out and will make provision for an evaluation of progress. The plan for forest fuel production, which will be part of the plan for the forest sector, should therefore be carried out by an economist working either directly to the country's planning department and in liason with the forest department or vice versa.

The main objectives of forest energy planning

These should be designed to meet a defined part or all of the long-term domestic fuel needs of the people from the forest resource, and to supply fuel for industrial use and export where comparative advantage could be shown to exist.

Evaluation of demand

Self-sufficiency in the basic foods and fuel is a reasonable aim for all governments irrespective of the comparative advantage which particular countries may enjoy in the production of certain goods and services. Food and fuel are bulky in relation to their market value and cannot be expected to carry heavy overhead costs (this point is especially relevant to fuelwood).

Fuel, food, and certain other products needed for clothing and shelter, are indispensable to man's survival and their continued supply should be the major concern of planners. The amount of fuel needed varies with the climate, the cooking habits of the people, and the family size. The basic *per capita* requirements of fuelwood must be determined by survey. An amount between 0·5–2·5 cubic metres per annum, i.e. 0·22–1·09 tonnes CE, is likely to apply to most regions where people depend upon wood as the prime domestic energy source.

Plans for the supply of forest fuel must be based upon forecasts of expected demand to ensure that long-term domestic needs are not jeopardized by industries established to utilize as raw material the wood which is needed for fuel and charcoal. Demand forecasts projected from consumer surveys carried out in a base period should take into account the various factors expected to affect the future consumption of a particular fuel; for example, growth in population and GNP may directly increase the demand for energy but substitution, price increase because of forest destruction, and consumer preference may decrease the demand for forest fuels. The difference between the two trends will be the net growth factor. The expected demand for forest fuel may then be calculated from the formula

$$D_t = D(1 + a)^t,$$

where D is the demand at present, D_t the demand in t years, and a the net growth factor.

Provided that the domestic fuel needs of the people can be met from existing and projected energy sources, planning can be undertaken with the aim of increasing the supply of fuel to serve industrial and export markets taking into account the opportunity cost of the raw material for other industrial use. The share of the market likely to be taken up by forest fuel can be increased by legislative action but if the advantages are made known such action should be unnecessary.

The effective demand for forest fuels in industry is relatively price-elastic because of the availability and convenience of alternative fuels, e.g. kerosene. There is strong evidence that a potential for expansion of demand for forest fuel, especially charcoal, exists in many parts of the world because the inelasticity of demand for energy is likely to favour the renewable fuels as market and political forces increase the relative prices of competitive energy sources.

Before an oil or gas company starts to sell in a country, it sets up a research and information centre in order to inform potential customers of all the advantages (and possibly some disadvantages) of using the products; this approach has not been applied to the marketing of forest fuel. Facts on its chemical and physical properties as well as the statistical information mentioned previously must be advertised in order that adequate knowledge of its possible uses and availability can be readily understood by industrialists and exporters. Only with adequate knowledge of the opportunities available for all forest-based fuels would an economist be able to produce a feasibility study to determine whether the investment potential would be large enough to attract the necessary capital. The power of advertising was well illustrated in Uganda where demonstrations, open days, broadcasts, and newspaper articles and other publicity arranged by the Forest Department served to increase the annual consumption of charcoal in 1971 to 63 700 tonnes, ten times the figure for 1967 (6000 tonnes). For a locally-based forest fuel industry to succeed in gaining the maximum benefit from an expansion of markets for energy, the potential consumer must be aware that charcoal and fuelwood, for example, are available in sufficient quantities at guaranteed qualities and at reasonable and stable prices. This means that the entrepreneur must be prepared to establish a reputation for reliability. In developing countries the achievement of continuity of supply is commonly the weakest link in the chain, for industrialists will be less easily persuaded to use forest fuel if it is felt that the future supply is likely to be erratic or uncertain. Much can be done in developing countries, where imperfect market conditions exist, by the state, which can help with marketing by introducing minimum recommended standards of quality and packaging and by imposing controlled prices. These measures will lead to consumer confidence and consequent expansion of the market.

Although it may not be economically practicable to use the entire surplus of forest increment as fuel for internal industrial expansion in a country, it may still be reasonable to manufacture charcoal, for example, on a commercial scale for export. If this were done, most of the economic and social advantages which arise from manufacturing charcoal in rural areas would be obtained. Sometimes further benefits may accrue from secondary conversion (e.g. briquetting or activation) in central industrial areas, but the first commitment should always be to the needs of the nationals of the producing country before entering into export contracts. Some analysis of import needs would also be desirable, since their extent would suggest what the level of exports (including charcoal) should be in order to earn the required foreign exchange.

The assessment of available resources

This will take into account the amount of wood available from existing forests and also the land which could be made available for fuel plantations. The factors that determine the extent of a country's land area that should be devoted to forestry are broadly considered by King (1968) to be controlled by the present and future supply of, and demand for, production, protection, and recreation. King suggests that only when goals for these goods and services have been ascertained can the area needed to meet these ends be calculated. Land requirements of other sectors of the economy must be considered in order that forestry projects may be accommodated in the framework of the whole economy.

It has been pointed out by MacGregor (1972) that the proportion of land under forests is a most inadequate guide to what the optimum size of the forest estate should be, since the extent to which a country devotes land to forestry should take into account the comparative advantage of exporting timber as well as serving home demand. There are many countries where certain raw materials exist in such profusion that their export may, with advantage, be encouraged in order to obtain capital for the establishment of local participation in industries without having to buy expensive technical assistance. This reasoning could apply very well to those tropical countries with low populations and high forest cover, where the great need is not necessarily to obtain the value added from conversion of timber but to ensure that the local demand for timber and fuel is met and that the price of timber exported is high enough to give a good return after all costs, including those of ensuring replacement of the crop, have been taken into account.

Many management decisions are based on reconciliation of alternatives which conflict with one another and are variously affected by restrictions. The most profitable course of action is therefore not often immediately apparent. Provided that there is a straight-line relationship between the various possible procedures and the realization of a simple objective, such as the maximization of NDR under conditions of financial constraint, linear programming can help to solve the complex problems associated with the best available mix of activities. An example of practical application to the problem of land allocation in forestry would be one which, with a given set of financial and other constraints, involved deciding how much forest should be left for natural regeneration; how much to enrich, cf. the Mengo System (Earl 1968 and Chapters 4 and 6); and how much to replant completely. Wardle (1964) explains how situations too complex to be solved by inspection or simple computation can be capable of solution by linear programming. The technique will also give information about variation of the optimum programme and changes in restrictions on the programme, which may provide critical guidance on the direction which management should take.

If maximization of the provision of forest fuel is set as one of the nation's goals and the demand forecasts for energy have been made, the necessary factors which are relevant to the satisfaction of this demand must be considered. The sustained supply of forest fuel depends upon the incremental product of the forest estate, which may be insufficient to provide for the future fuel needs. The appraisal of the total fuel requirements of a country will take into account the various parameters discussed in Chapter 5 and from these it is possible to calculate the amount of land to be devoted to fuel production and how it should be distributed in relation to the future fuel needs of population and the centres of industry. The existing forest areas may be capable of yielding a sustained supply of fuel from thinnings and refining operations or from the residues from final fellings. The amount available should be calculated for each district and the effective and potential demand for forest products required by any possible competing industries measured. The difference between the calculated supply of fuel available from existing sources and the amount required, as shown by the demand forecasts, will have to be provided from other sources. If the policy is to provide for part or all of this deficit from the land resource, an appraisal of the productivity of various suitable tree species upon the sites available should be undertaken. The results of this productivity analysis can be applied to the following formula to arrive at the area of land required in order to meet the production target.

$$A = D - \frac{S}{I},$$

where A is the area to be devoted to growing the forecasted annual requirement of fuel, D the estimated annual requirements of fuel determined by demand forecasts to the end of the forecasted period, S the forecast of sustainable annual supply of fuel from existing sources, and I the mean annual increment over the minimum rotation period to obtain the size of material required (determined by productivity analysis).

The use of the formula assumes that the maximization of fuel production is the sole criterion and that any policy decision which may affect the achievement of this aim, e.g. timber production, protection, amenity, recreation, and conservation, should be applied as constraints to I. If the demand forecasts indicate that an increasing or decreasing share of the requirement with need to be filled by forest fuel $(D - S)$, or that the amount of fuel likely to be available from other sources S shows a positive or negative trend, an appropriate time series, possibly combined with a network analysis for the district or country, should be compiled in order to provide for the release or acquisition of plantable land at the right stages. Land used for growing fuel has an opportunity cost which must be taken into account when making planning decisions but if the provision of forest fuel is regarded as a social function of the state through the medium of the forest department, an expected financial return from fuel plantations approaching the marginal cost of capital should be sufficient justification for the establishment of fuel plantation schemes. The economic or social rate of return would be normally expected to be much higher.

The assessment of ways of meeting the objectives

The assessment is probably better made from the bottom up rather than from the top down because of the different local conditions which are likely to affect the approach. In developing countries the supply of forest energy to towns and industries will probably be either as fuelwood or charcoal; the forest department will be responsible for growing the raw materials and will probably have to become involved in the production and marketing organization where entrepreneurial ability is deficient. The choice between fuelwood or charcoal depends very much upon the distance between the forest and the market. Charcoal is much more complicated to produce and organize and will probably benefit from a charcoal development section being set up as part of the utilization activities of the forest department. A full account of the ways in which this may be accomplished has been given by Earl (1973a).

The planning of the supply of fuelwood and charcoal will be the function of the district forest officers, who would be required to calculate the planting and felling requirements for various markets as shown in the following example.

Area of forest required to supply charcoal in Uganda

(1) Town of 8000 persons

(a) *Eucalyptus saligna* plantation

$$\frac{8000 \times 0{\cdot}3 \times 6}{15} = 960 \text{ ha}$$

(b) Tropical high forest

$$\frac{8000 \times 0{\cdot}3 \times 6}{3} = 4800 \text{ ha}$$

(2) Smelter 100 000 tonnes pig iron per annum

(a) *Eucalyptus saligna*

$$\frac{100\,000 \times 0{\cdot}7 \times 6}{15} = 28\,000 \text{ ha}$$

(b) Tropical high forest

$$\frac{100\,000 \times 0{\cdot}7 \times 6}{3} = 140\,000 \text{ ha}$$

Increment *Eucalyptus saligna*	15 m^3/ha/an 7 year rotation
Increment tropical high forest	3 m^3/ha/an 35 year rotation plus 6 m^3/ha/an quality timber
Conversion rate wood/charcoal	6 m^3/tonne
Conversion rate charcoal/iron	0·7 tonnes charcoal/tonne iron
Domestic consumption charcoal	300 kg *per capita*

N.B. The supply of charcoal from extensive tropical high forest would be cheaper as the raw material would be produced as a result of refining operations designed to improve the yield of timber (see Chapter 4) and not from plantations established especially for the purpose.

If the existing arrangements for supplying the market are adequate, the local forest officers may merely issue licences to local entrepreneurs to cut and sell fuelwood or manufacture and market charcoal in their districts. It is essential that the forest department, which supplies the wood, should make sure that the entrepreneurs are working in the public interest by strictly controlling what they may or not cut.

Selection of suitable projects

If a dynamic approach is taken, the provision of fuel to meet the future needs of an industry may need radical changes in methods and market organization and should be subjected to the discipline of project planning using economic criteria. On occasion the demand for forest fuel may go well beyond the resources of the existing forests, for example, when massive amounts of charcoal are required for a charcoal—iron industry. Here it may be necessary to carry out feasibility studies to avoid spending money on the appraisal of impracticable projects. Where projects are found to be technically feasible an appraisal should be made in order to ascertain whether or not they are both economically and socially sound. A suggested sequence of stages which may be followed in project appraisals is as follows.

(1) Study of project objectives and alternatives;
(2) social cost—benefit analysis (including sensitivity and risk analysis);
(3) commercial and financial analysis;
(4) other economic considerations;
(5) conclusions and recommendations.

There are several manuals of project appraisal which provide useful case studies for assisting the economist making the analysis, for example, *A guide to project appraisal in developing countries* (O.D.A. 1972); a convenient check-list is given by Watt (1972).

Planning for the supply of forest energy does not normally extend beyond the physical boundaries of the forest as far as the forest department authorities are concerned, although in many countries para-statal organizations, such as the National Fuel Corporation in Nepal, are concerned with marketing as well as the purchase and transport of fuelwood. In those countries with a large, urban demand the collection and carriage of fuel to central markets could with advantage be organized by a para-statal organization and might thereby qualify for loans. Occasionally large private corporations grow their own fuel in plantations. In Uganda some of the sugar companies and the multi-national tobacco company grow Eucalyptus on a 5—7 year rotation in close co-operation with the Forest Department; the tobacco company provides finance and a guaranteed market for the fuel produced by the farmers growing the tobacco and the forest department supplies technical experts on secondment terms and the plants. In both developed and developing countries the supply of large quantities of fuelwood to power stations or charcoal to blast furnaces requires a great deal of detailed planning if it is to succeed. Projects requiring huge inputs of wood are often proposed by industrialists or business interests who have no idea of the ecological, silvicultural, or sociological problems involved. Occasionally these interests may have full government backing before the forest department is approached but provided that the proposed projects are economically and socially desirable and do not conflict with the development aims of the country, the forest department concerned should welcome them if it has power to enforce the conditions that are necessary to ensure that the country's forest wealth is not diminished. The assessment of the value of a number of projects which may be mutually exclusive to one another requires the application of social cost—benefit analysis in order to ensure that the long-term interests of the people are not prejudiced by the financial attractiveness of a short-term gain.

Implementation of projects

This depends upon entrepreneurship, both private and state. Much rests with the character and personalities of the businessmen and forest officers of the country concerned. Provided that the project falls within the general framework of acceptability, the choice of how much private and how much state participation is considered to be desirable is a matter for the politicians.

Case-study of planning for the supply of domestic fuel to settlers in a district of Nepal

Planning for the supply of forest fuel in a locality requires political action and an appreciation of the wider issues involved as well as good local knowledge. The need for factual information before planning can take place may be illustrated by a case-study example of the calculations necessary to estimate the fuelwood area needed in a district of Nepal.

The land area which has the greatest potential contribution to solving both the fuel and food problem in Nepal is the flat alluvial plain bordering India, known as the Terai (see Fig. 7.1). In the Bardia district of the Terai the Government-owned Nepal Settlement Company is clearing the forest and settling people at the rate of one family per holding of 2·7 hectares. Until 1974 no provision had been made for retaining forest for fuel and other basic essentials. When there is no more forest debris to burn the settlers are faced with the problem of finding fuel from the receding forest resource or obtaining alternative fuels. As commercial sources of fuel are scarce and expensive the net result is that the settlers are eventually forced to burn dung. It is unlikely that electric power will be available to most Nepalese people for a long time because of price and the inherent difficulties in bringing power to dispersed populations. An additional problem is that the local population, the Tharu, has traditionally regarded the forest as a ready source of fuel. The influence of state-encouraged immigration upon the availability of fuelwood, which will result in clearing forest for agriculture and increase total fuelwood consumption, will be to reduce the standard of living formerly enjoyed by the indigenous people and will eventually eliminate the fuel resource altogether unless measures are taken to safeguard future supplies.

The objective is to ensure a sustained supply of fuelwood for the settlement scheme. Demand studies have established that the *per capita* consumption of fuelwood in 1970 in the Terai was about 1·0 cubic metres as opposed to 0·5 cubic metres elsewhere in Nepal (Chapter 5). It is assumed that the *per capita* consumption

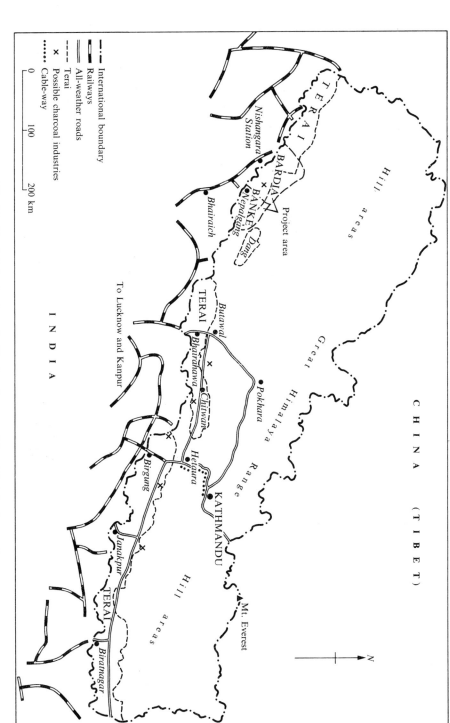

Fig. 7.1. Nepal: infrastructure, the Terai, and proposed forest fuel development areas

of fuelwood in the Terai will progressively decrease until it falls to the level of 0·5 cubic metres found elsewhere in the hills and mountains of Nepal, where fuel is scarce and people are forced to be thrifty. Estimates of the decreasing *per capita* fuelwood consumption in Nepal for 1980, 1990, and 2000 are shown in Table A.8 (p. 113); these take into account the increasing marginal utility of fuelwood leading to greater economy in usage as the forests of the Terai are cut over and the resource becomes scarcer throughout the country. An assessment of the land required for the provision of fuel has been made using the information gained from the Forest Department and the F.A.O. Forest Project at Bardia and from the demand studies shown in Chapter 5.

TABLE 7.1

Data needed for an assessment of land required for the provision of fuel in the Bardia district of the Terai

Population of Bardia district in 1972	104 428
Estimated average population growth rate until 1980 (allowing for immigration;	4½%
Population in 1980 (estimated)	148 507
Estimated average growth rate between 1980 and 1990	3½%
Estimated average growth rate between 1990 and 2000	2½%
Amount of forest cleared in order to settle 1000 families per annum	2700 ha/annum
Estimated consumption of fuelwood *per capita* per annum with forest freely available but no settlement clearing	$1·0 \text{ m}^3$
Estimated basic minimum requirements of fuelwood *per capita* per annum	$0·5 \text{ m}^3$
Average amount of fuelwood per hectare from forest clearing	75 m^3
Amount of fuelwood available each year from clearing (estimated)	$2700 \times 75 = 202\ 500 \text{ m}^3$
Equivalent to a *per capita* consumption of Declining to	$1·94 \text{ m}^3$ in 1972 $1·36 \text{ m}^3$ in 1980
Amount of fuelwood available from refining operations in the managed forest in Bardia (estimated)	2660 m^3/annum
Increment of fuelwood portion of natural forest (estimated)	$2·5 \text{ m}^3$/ha/annum
Increment of Eucalyptus plantation	$20·0 \text{ m}^3$/ha/annum

After the settlement scheme terminates, possibly in 1980, there will be no more fuelwood supplies available from the liquidation of forest capital, and the amount consumed in 1980 will be 118 806 m³ (the *per capita* requirement is estimated at 0·80 m³, see Table A.8, multiplied by the population 148 507). It can therefore be assumed that in 1981 the stocks of fuel available for use by the newest holdings or available for sale to the others will be 202 500 − 118 806 = 83 694 cubic metres. The deficits in 1981, 1982, and 1983 will be as shown in Table 7.2.

TABLE 7.2

Calculation of fuelwood deficits for the Bardia settlement area, Nepal

Year	(Population × fuel needs/caput)−stocks		Deficit m³
1981	$(153\ 705 \times 0\cdot78) - (83\ 694 + 2660)$	=	33 536
1982	$(159\ 085 \times 0\cdot76) - 2660$	=	118 244
1983	$(164\ 653 \times 0\cdot74) - 2660$	=	119 183

After 1983 there is an estimated forecasted future increase of approximately 2 per cent per annum because of population increase.

Assuming that state organized settlement ceases in 1980, the area of natural forest needed to supply the amount of fuel required for the district in 1981 from increment would be $33\ 536/2\cdot5 = 13\ 414$ hectares. In 1982 the amount required would rise to $118\ 244/2\cdot5 = 47\ 298$ hectares. ($118\ 244/20 = 5912$ hectares if Eucalyptus plantations are established and cut on a 7-year rotation.)

The two main demand shifters for fuelwood after 1982, when the demand will have become stabilized, are likely to be the expected expansion in population and the fall in *per capita* consumption because of increasing scarcity and higher prices. These would result in a combined effective increase in demand of 2 per cent per annum, which might well be allowed for by an area of forest left for contingencies. The most practical solution to the problem of how much forest to reserve for fuelwood production is to assume that the full amount of natural forest will be required, say 50 000 hectares (including a contingency allowance) and to allow for the transfer of forest at a later date to alternative use in proportion to the amount placed under intensive management for fuel. Thus, for every 100 hectares planted with Eucalyptus, 700 hectares could be released for other use.

An assessment of the most practical means of meeting future fuel needs shows clearly that planning for the time when the settlement ceases should begin now and it should be so arranged as to allow portions of natural forest or plantations to be distributed among the farmlands to avoid haulage problems and to provide for recreation and conservation. The allocation of land for forest should be made using the basic formula on p. 91; thus for every 2700 hectares of forest cleared for 1000 families (average size 7) the amount of forest to be left should be $7000/2\cdot5 \times 0\cdot5 = 1400$ hectares: enough to supply the minimum requirement of fuelwood of 0·5 cubic metres from 0·2 hectares *per capita*. If, however, it were decided that the opportunity cost of the land that would have to be left for natural forest in order to supply enough fuel for the settled families was too high, and it were agreed to plant Eucalyptus immediately, the area of land which should be reserved annually for fuel could be reduced to $7000/20 \times 0\cdot5 = 175$ hectares. Assuming that it were not possible to plant 175 hectares per annum with Eucalyptus, the area of forest needed for fuel for the families already settled would be calculated as follows.

Total requirement of forest for fuel 1980	50 000 ha
Amount of forest to be reserved for fuel for settlers between 1972–80 (1400 × 8)	11 200 ha
Amount of forest required for settlers already settled	38 800 ha

The need for fuel in the Bardia District is so pressing that there should be no difficulty in obtaining support for a suitable project which could translate theory into results. One way would be for the Forest Department to take over the management of the forest left for fuel reserves and for a forester to be appointed in charge of fuel preparation, sales, and replanting. The alternative would be for the fuel-cutting and sales to be the function of private enterprise or a co-operative, with the Forest Department allocating areas for felling and obtaining a royalty for the produce which should be used for management. The problem is not difficult to solve if plans are made to ensure that part of the forest is reserved for future fuel needs. It is then easy to prepare for the time when fuel will not be available at a low price within the area.

The settlement scheme, so far, has made no provision of any kind for future fuelwood supplies and it is likely that, if nothing is done soon, the people will resort to raiding the managed forest for wood on an hitherto unprecedented scale. The effect of this planning inaction would be to cause local hardship and the loss of a national asset by the ultimate destruction of the remaining managed forest.

The effects of lack of planning at a later stage were noted at Janakpur in the Eastern Terai, where most of the trees have been cut and burnt for about 35 kilometres distance from the town and people have to walk for several days to the forest and back to obtain fuel. The nearest forest at Sagarnath-Gausala is being stripped and destroyed as a result of the insatiable demand for fuel. The forest staff find it practically impossible to halt the removal of fuelwood from the forest and the more serious cutting down of valuable young timber species. The fuel shortage at Janakpur is aggravated by the demand for fuelwood for the 450 tobacco barns in the area, which consume 7600 tonnes of fuelwood per annum. The annual consumption of fuelwood for the barns is expected to rise to 10 000 tonnes by 1976 and since even the mango fruit trees are being sacrificed for fuel the area is rapidly becoming a semi-desert. These conditions are being worsened by the substitution of cow dung, formerly returned to the land, for fuel. The deteriorating situation at Janakpur can be directly attributed to the lack of earlier planning.

It was stated by Sinden in an unpublished report (1971) that the importance of fuelwood to the Nepalese people should be a constraint on any future land-use planning in the Terai. That this is not being taken into account is serious for the people, who appear to be deluded into the belief that the fuel, which they have always regarded as a social good, will still be available even as the trees give way to crops and urban development.

It is clear that the problem is vast and might be partly solved if alternative energy supplies become available. This possibility has been excluded from the analysis because of lack of information but should be included in any thorough-going investigation of the area. It is, however, doubtful whether much more than a small part of the total energy needs of the area would be likely to be met by fossil fuel or electricity, at least for the period of time covered by this study.

An example of good planning in India

An example of a well-planned joint enterprise between industry and the Forest Department is taken from Mysore, India. A blast furnace industry with an output of 80 tonnes of iron per day, together with a ferro-silicon plant, is supplied with 40 000 tonnes of charcoal per annum from the surrounding forests. Formerly the charcoal was made from distillation of fuelwood in the plant but in 1968 it was decided to stop this method of manufacture on economic grounds and to buy all charcoal from the Forest Department at an agreed price negotiated each year (average U.S. $26 per tonne in 1971–2).

Approximately 3200–4000 hectares of lightly-exploited, low-value natural forest is cleared annually for conversion to plantation. The Forest Department, which organizes and administers the whole process, receives a royalty of U.S. $0·125 per bag (i.e. U.S. $3·75 per tonne of approximately 30 bags) from the charcoal converted from the felled scrub. The operation is well organized to ensure that all the cleared land is planted with trees during the wet season when there is a temporary lull in the charcoal-making operations and men are available for the task. The work takes place in various State forests and is closely tied-in with forest management requirements. The operations in Aramballi State Forest near the village of Muithinakoppa, approximately 40 kilometres south of Bhadravati, are typical of those carried out elsewhere. The basic organization of the work in 1972 was as follows.

(1) Timber trees are felled and removed to the government depot, at the rate of approximately 127 cubic metres per hectare, for auction.
(2) The Forest Department calls for tenders for the manufacture of charcoal from the lop and top and all remaining trees in the demarcated area of forest, and transport to the Bhadravati Iron and Steel Works. The price is U.S. $0·50 per bag i.e. U.S. $15·0 per tonne ex tax and royalty.
(3) Charcoal is made, on contract, in large earth kilns. The contractor pays the charcoal-makers U.S. $0·25 per bag stacked ready for loading on to a lorry.
(4) The amount of charcoal per hectare is about 20–25 tonnes i.e. 600–750 bags.
(5) Approximately 120 men are employed on charcoal-making in the dry season of 6–8 months and plant trees for the Forest Department at a daily rate of U.S. $0·31 in the wet season, i.e. for the remaining months.
(6) 75 per cent of the area is planted with Eucalyptus (*E. tereticornis*) and the remainder is planted with Teak (*Tectona grandis*), Silky Oak (*Grevillea robusta*), and She Oak (*Casuarina* species).

(7) Planting costs are about U.S. $41 per hectare for Eucalyptus planted at
1·5 × 1·5 metres spacing and *Tectona* at 1·8 × 1·8 metres spacing.

The royalty to the Forest Department of U.S. $70–90 per hectare is more
than the planting costs of U.S. $41 per hectare and demonstrates the important
role played in development by the use of fuel obtained as a by-product from
intelligently-planned forest operations.

In Mysore good planning has ensured work for 5000 persons on charcoal alone
in the forest and at the same time provided the Forest Department with the means
of improving its forests. The danger is that charcoal might be priced out of the
market because of the availability of low-grade but cheap coal, although there is
no doubt that charcoal is much better for smelting than coal or coke. The price
should be kept under constant review and if it unavoidably rises too far above
that of coal or coke it might be necessary for the Forest Department to lower its
royalty in order to retain this market, which has very important economic benefits
for forestry as well as other social benefits. A further fear is that the supplies of
charcoal will eventually diminish, and it is suggested that the Forest Department
should allocate some Eucalyptus areas to charcoal production in order to keep
the market and ensure continuity of supply. In 1974, the Indian five-year plan
had been completely upset by the increase in the price of oil from U.S. $4 to
more than U.S. $10 per barrel; this makes it highly unlikely that low-priced coal
will be available to supplant charcoal in the long term.

Common features of some developing countries

A common characteristic of developing countries is a low commercial energy
consumption, a high forest energy consumption, and a large, but rapidly
decreasing, forest resource. A comparison is made in Table 7.3 between three
countries (see Earl 1971, 1972a, 1973b). In each of these countries there is great
difficulty in finding enough money to pay for silvicultural management of the
forest. The consequences are that vast areas of natural forest are being 'mined'
for timber and the opportunity for increasing their potential to provide for timber
and for fuel in the future at marginal cost has been irretrievably lost. The lack of
infrastructure is a constraint to development but road and rail links are rapidly
being improved and expanded through forest areas which could be made to contribute to energy supplies. It has been demonstrated that the use of portable steel
kilns for converting waste wood to charcoal is economically sound where road
and rail links between the forests and the towns have been established. It is
estimated that out of the annual cut of 290 000 hectares, 4 million tonnes of
charcoal could be salvaged annually from the wood left behind after exploitation
of the Ivory Coast's forests and substantial amounts from the forests of
Madagascar and Nepal. Provided that the necessary planning were undertaken, a
small part of the revenue obtained from fuelling operations would pay for the
rehabilitation and enrichment of enough of these forests to ensure the continued
supply of timber and fuel in the future.

TABLE 7.3

A comparison of the salient features affecting forest energy consumption in three developing countries (1971)

	Ivory Coast	Madagascar	Nepal
Land area (million ha)	32	59	14
Forest area (million ha)	6·3	12	4
Percentage forest	19·7	20·4	28·6
Population (million)	5·2	7·2	11·3
Persons per ha	0·16	0·12	0·81
Forest area (ha *per capita*)	1·2	1·7	0·4
GNP *per capita* U.S. $.	330	140	90
Fossil fuel resources	Nil	Nil	Nil
Hydro-electric potential	Some	Some	Vast
Commercial energy consumption (kg CE/*caput*/an)	180	64	11
Forest energy consumption (kg CE/*caput*/an)	438	240	248
Forest industry	Round logs exported	Some round logs exported	Some round logs exported

Planning for posterity

Planning is essential for the protection of finite and the creation of renewable resources. The forest is a resource which, it has long been recognized, cannot be left to market forces to control without the proliferation of undesirable externalities. Planning, by adequate reservation of areas of forest for the future fuel requirements of the people, can ensure that the full benefits of land clearance and settlement are not lost. New developments including reservoirs, hydro-electric schemes and new infrastructural links usually involve clearing and burning forests. If well-planned, the unmerchantable trees could be put to good use by converting them to charcoal and storing the fuel until required instead of allowing a vast loss of energy to take place. For the long-term benefit of the people, governments must ensure that there is sufficient fuel at a price that consumers can afford. Planning will give guidance to the policy-makers on how this can be wholly or partly maintained from the renewable forest resource, a resource which has great potential for raising the material and cultural standards of mankind and for ensuring that the environment is safeguarded for the benefit of succeeding generations.

8 Future prospects

'Come my friends,
'Tis not too late to seek a newer world . . .
Though much is taken, much remains; and though
We are not now that strength which in old days
Moved earth and heaven, that which we are, we are;
One equal temper of heroic hearts
Made weak by time and fate, but strong in will,
To strive, to seek, to find, and not to yield.'

Tennyson, *Ulysses*

The world is moving into an era where the effects of the depletion of finite resources must be taken into account in the economic analysis of long-term development. This is a completely different situation from that which existed when
economic development was commencing in the U.S.A. and other now developed
countries. As GNP and consumption of energy are almost linearly related, the
effects of the present pattern of growth of both national product and population
on global energy consumption are obvious. The effect of an increase in GNP in a
developing country upon the global consumption of energy is, however, only
marginal when compared with the consumption in developed economies (see
Table 8.1) but the effect of rapid population increase upon the consumption of
energy in a developing country is of prime importance for its own economy.

TABLE 8.1
Annual commercial energy consumption for some selected countries

Country	Commercial energy consumption 1970	Increase in energy consumption for a 5% economic growth rate
	(kg CE *per capita*)	
United States	10 774	539·0
United Kingdom	5139	257·0
Malawi	41	2·0
Nepal	11	0·5

Source: U.N. (1971)

The high population pressure in the developing countries is the biggest single
factor that hinders the raising of their standard of living. Developing countries
will require a greater share of the world's energy resources than they have so far

commanded if they are to achieve economic independence, but it is unlikely that countries without indigenous fossil fuels will be able to pay for all the energy imports that they deem to be essential.

Economic growth in developed countries has become dependent upon increasing inputs of finite energy resources. If this trend continues and the transfer from renewable to non-renewable fuels in developing countries is encouraged, substantial price rises in fossil fuels will result or the remaining non-renewable energy resources will be rapidly depleted, with the consequent risk of serious shortages of fossil fuels for chemical feedstocks and for energy purposes in the near future. Alternative sources of power from hydro-electric schemes and nuclear power stations are unlikely to affect the general trend towards dearer energy in the short run because of the vast capital investment they require. The price of nuclear fuel is, moreover, already showing signs of rising in response to the increasing demand for energy.

It is particularly dangerous for developing countries to rely upon trends which have occurred in the present developed countries. Oil resources are being depleted at a much faster rate than formerly, and this is certain to lead to substantial price increases, not only for oil but for all its substitutes. Although developed countries with adequate funds will utilize their 'consumer surplus' to purchase fuel for their expanding energy needs, the outlook for developing countries is bleak, since substitution is realistic only for those countries which can afford the substitutes.

The theory of substitution is that the exploitation of resources can be expanded indefinitely, given high enough market prices, until the level is reached for substitution to take place; for example, as ores containing a metal become scarce, the price of the metal will rise until it reaches the level at which it becomes economic to utilize poorer ores or to substitute alternative products. Similarly it is argued that as crude oil becomes scarce and the price increases it will become economic to extract or synthesize oil from shale, tar sands, or coal. Modern economic thinking recognizes the part that market forces can play in encouraging the search for alternative materials but realizes that the validity of the substitution theory depends upon the availability of an increasing supply of energy for the extraction processes, for the lower the concentration of the required product in a resource, the higher are the energy inputs required for extraction. In order to calculate the energy cost of exploiting a resource, the total energy expended at each stage in mining and refining is divided by the quantity of product finally obtained to obtain an energy cost per unit. For example, for a copper ore containing 2 per cent metal, the ore processes require about 6 kWh per kilogram of copper, and the metal-refining processes contribute about 16 kilowatt-hours per kilogram, thus giving a total of 22 kWh per kilogram of copper. Hence starting with a 1 per cent ore, the ore processes will require about 12 kWh per kilogram and the total energy cost would rise to 28 kilowatt-hours per kilogram of copper (Chapman 1973).

An understanding of the Second Law of Thermodynamics will lead to a realization of the complete dependence of every economic process upon the availability of energy and will help to focus attention upon the long-term planning needed to solve the economic and developmental problems which will be posed by the depletion of the fossil fuel resources.

If an increase in economic growth, in the terms of the criteria used since the exploitation of the fossil fuel resource began, is deemed to be necessary to modern life, large and increasing supplies of energy will be needed to sustain the present social and economic structure of civilization. Energy from nuclear fission cannot be relied upon to fill the gap without the risk of damage to the environment because the problem of how to dispose of highly dangerous radio-active wastes has not been satisfactorily solved. It is still not certain that nuclear fusion can be harnessed commercially and unlikely that energy from this source could contribute anything to the world economy before A.D. 2000.

Renewable energy resources offer considerable hope for increasing the annual energy take-off without jeopardizing the future of mankind by producing harmful externalities. Although the amount of renewable energy used at present is only a low proportion of the total energy budget, the potential is enormous and the utilized fraction can be expected to expand rapidly if sufficient attention is paid to the technological problems involved. Electricity from hydro-electric, geothermal, tidal, and direct solar sources, together with the renewable fuel resources, offer opportunities for supplementing the remaining fossil fuel reserves until such time as nuclear fuel can play a part in supplying energy safely. Political arguments are involved in the decision-making but no lowering of safety standards, when dealing with radioactivity, is worth considering on grounds of expediency. The environmental and social costs of having nuclear power stations in most areas of natural beauty, for safety reasons, have not yet entered into the calculations but when this is done the total costs of relying on nuclear power may be seen to be far too high.

The development of the renewable forest fuel source

For many purposes fuel (stored energy) is needed, and power obtained from continuous processes is difficult and expensive to store in a suitable form.

This book has been constructed upon the proposition that forests have a potential for the provision of renewable supplies of fuel in much greater quantities than has hitherto been realized, which could be used for economic and social development. The establishment of the proposition has been reached from facts obtained from basic research; and it has become apparent that apart from the observable practical benefits obtainable from the use of forest energy, there are less immediately obvious indirect benefits arising from such applications which have particular significance for developing countries and are also significant for the future economic and social development of the world as a whole.

The technical disadvantage of fuelwood lies in its bulk, which when accompanied by comparative inaccessibility increases its cost to a level at which alternative fuels may have the advantage. Sometimes the solution lies in the conversion of the primary wood source to secondary fuels with properties appropriate to the desired end-use. The costs of fossil fuel are now rising so fast as to encourage the use of forest fuel in countries that are ill-prepared to sustain supplies, therefore action must be taken if loss of forests on a vast scale is to be avoided.

The opportunity costs of forest conversion

The amount of energy fixed annually by vegetation is very large but it is only through the application of sound agricultural, ecological, and silvicultural principles that fuelwood can be provided in sustained quantities of the desired quality. The developing countries have among them the greatest untapped energy potential in their forests, which if managed well could supply all their energy requirements and provide a surplus for export. The development and use of this energy resource could substantially increase the long-term prospects for economic and social improvement of many countries.

Wood when burned as fuel has an opportunity cost which varies according to the economic situation of a country and the location of the forest. It should consequently not be used as fuel if an alternative application, which leaves the resource in a lower entropy state, is available. The forest is a resource which can be managed to provide for a multiplicity of needs with almost no direct finite resource cost at all, for example, there are many forests which could be managed to enable one part of the increment to be harvested as timber and the other part as fuel in the conversion process.

Because of the uneven distribution of fuel and power resources in the world, some countries will not be able to obtain sufficient supplies of energy for development without the sacrifice of a disproportionately high percentage of their other natural resources. This is particularly serious for developing countries, which do not have the comparative advantage of being able to produce goods and services required by the nations with a surplus of energy.

More than half the world's population depends upon wood for cooking and heating purposes and the domestic fuel needs of those people must always be taken into account when drawing up development schemes involving changes in traditional land-use. In many countries the forest lands are being converted to other forms of use without any calculation of the opportunity cost of the energy lost as a result of the change in land-use. One of the purposes of this book is to indicate to those concerned with land-planning that forests are valuable as a source of renewable energy. In a number of developing countries, including Brazil, the Central African Republic, East Africa, India, Ivory Coast, Madagascar, Nepal and Sri Lanka, the potential for the development of forest fuel resources is vast, but governments are often not aware of the benefits it is possible to obtain from their own forest resources. At the present time, although 90 per cent of all timber consumed in developing countries is burnt as fuel, it is estimated that fuel equivalent to 3500 million tonnes of coal could be available from the unused annual increment. This fuel source, much of which could be used for development, is more than half the annual total consumption of energy from non-forest sources for the world. The factors inhibiting the fuller exploitation of this energy are less attributable to economic and technical causes than to the fact that there is usually no suitable institutional support for building-up an industry in the transition from a domestic to a market economy.

In many countries, for example, the Central African Republic, the Ivory Coast, Madagascar, and Nepal, the huge capital reserves of energy in the forests are being dissipated at an alarmingly high rate. The Ivory Coast forests are being exploited and converted to other uses at the rate of 290 000 hectares per annum. Apart from the 'once-and-for-all' foreign exchange earnings from the sale of round logs, no other benefit is received from the cut-over forest and the social benefits obtained from the availability of free fuelwood are being rapidly eroded. There is consequently a great need to point out to goverments the true costs of such destruction before it is too late.

The value of the forests as sources of the basic fuel requirements for more than half of the world's population is often forgotten by economists trained to respond to forces and disciplines imposed by market economies. It is particularly important to recognize that people's needs are not adequately represented by and may extend beyond a figure for GNP *per capita*. In developing countries modern and traditional economies frequently exist side by side. This economic dualism has not been re- duced in former colonial territories since independence and in some cases it has become firmly entrenched and takes the form of urban bias. Barber (1970), Lipton (1970), and Stewart (1972) have all contributed towards an understanding of this problem which has increased the maldistribution of resources in developing countries. Changes in land-use sometimes leave the subsistence villagers worse off because of an effective switch of resources from the poor of the traditional sector to the comparative rich of the modern sector.

The economic and social basis for forest management

In managed forests the provision of fuelwood and building poles is sometimes inhibited by the fact that silvicultural work usually aims to produce the maximum quantity of wood for industrial use and sometimes quality timber. For example, the management objectives contained in the working plan for Mengo District in Uganda, Webster (1961), state that 'The object of management is to produce in perpetuity the maximum quantity of high-grade timber from the forests by the most efficient methods, provided that the satisfaction of the needs of the inhabi- tants of Uganda must take precedence over export considerations.' The latter part of the statement is ambiguous: most people in Uganda cannot afford the luxury of high-grade timber but require poles and low-grade timber to make houses and furniture, and fuelwood for cooking their food.

The production of high-grade timber by the most efficient methods can be the primary object of management and, if well planned, still satisfy a variety of different claims on the forest. The reconciliation of various interests was achieved in Uganda by a system evolved for increasing the productivity of tropical forests at minimal cost by converting unwanted vegetation to charcoal and filling up the gaps thus created with 'desirable' trees (Earl 1968). This system was cheaper than poisoning, environmentally much more desirable, and provided benefits for all sections of the people.

The policy of replacing natural forests of low productivity by plantations with a greater propensity for growth accords with the basic aim of those who seek to make the best use of available resources but is often carried out without enough regard for environmental consequences. This narrow view of forestry management encourages the replacement of mixed forests by monocultures and may result in a loss of soil fertility and some of the social and amenity values of forests which foresters claim to uphold. Price (unpublished, 1971) has given a succinct account of some aspects of the social costs of an over-enthusiastic use of a single silvicultural criterion in British forestry. Where the opportunity cost of forest land is low and the marginal efficiency of the land factor is greater than that of other factor inputs, plantations may be less profitable than managed mixed forests, which can sometimes obviate the risk of serving sectarian or narrow interests to the detriment of the total return which could be enjoyed (Earl 1972b). Mixed forests, by their diversification, are capable of avoiding the risks of having all the eggs in one basket.

Financial analysis based upon the expected commercial returns from a tree crop should be used only for projects serving a particular industrial need and then only after taking into account direct social costs, e.g. the loss of 'free' building materials and fuelwood. For general application to national forestry undertakings, economic analysis should use the maximization of net social benefit criterion on the principle that land should serve the long-term as well as the immediate needs of the people. Many forests may not satisfy the rigours of a commercial analysis but may be justified in economic terms provided that an appraisal of all the benefits is undertaken; such appraisal may require the imputation of surrogate prices for the benefits of goods and services received from the forest free or at subsidized rates; for example, the assessment of productivity usually ignores fuelwood production if it is outside the market economy. No policy decisions can hope to optimize benefits unless they have taken into account all the facts. It is because some of the facts have not been taken into account when judging the usefulness of forests that decisions have been made which have subsequently been regretted.

The aid opportunity

Developed countries have recognized that there is an obligation for them to encourage the economic growth of the developing countries by providing financial and technical assistance. There are advantages to both recipient and donor countries from the flow of aid. The recipient country is able to acquire technology and to sell abroad or substitute home-produced products for imports and is thereby able to effect savings in foreign exchange. The donor country gains from the added experience of its nationals and from the non-discriminatory reduction of the barriers to international trade. Apart from assistance with staff, aid is usually tied to specific projects which are prepared by economists who use the maximization of NDR or other similar financial criteria as the yardsticks for comparison with other opportunities submitted by the governments to the aid agency.

The commercial basis to some aid schemes has served to create unnecessary cynicism about the use of 'aid' to promote development, for it commonly seems that the main tangible advantages obtained from aid are fringe benefits from expenditure of expatriate staff on such items as local food, furnishing, and employment of house servants.

Foreign involvement undoubtedly helps to relieve suffering and to induce growth, and if the word 'investment' were substituted for the word 'aid' where commercial returns to the donor country are expected, much misunderstanding could be avoided. It is important to give priority to aid which ensures that food and fuel from the land are in equilibrium with the population; for example by providing the means to increase basic crop yields and family planning services. People also want economic growth and provided that their basic requirements are not jeopardized by land-based projects which remove their source of food and fuel, investment in agricultural and rural enterprises for many countries is likely to be more rewarding both to investors and to the long-term development prospects of the countries concerned than investment in capital-intensive industrial enterprises. For example, developing the energy potential of forests by establishing charcoal-making enterprises would materially assist both the donor and the receiving nation and, in addition, would improve the long-term prospects for the world as a whole.

There is a unique opportunity of providing assistance which would help the inhabitants of developing countries by providing (1) aid in the form of technical assistance and financial help for planning their domestic fuel supplies, and (2) investment in projects to supply fuel for vertically integrated industry and export from managed multi-use forests and fuel plantations. Multi-lateral agencies might provide the aid needed for (1), bi-lateral and private sources could well take up the investment challenge provided by (2).

The energy challenge

A radical approach to the energy problem will be required from economists, technologists and aid agencies if the potential of the forest energy source for economic and social development is to be realized. It is hoped that, in addition to providing a theoretical background to a proposition, this book will serve to direct attention to the need for more research into the ways in which the long-term as well as the short-term energy needs of mankind can be met from forests.

If the thesis is accepted that forest fuel sources will provide an increasingly vital part of the future energy needs of man, then it is not too early to begin planning now. The vastness of the problem, its importance, and its immediate relevance to the problems of the developing world make the subject ideally suited for co-operation between the developed and developing countries through bilateral and multilateral aid projects.

Appendix 1: Fuelwood in Nepal

Calculation of the present and future consumption of fuelwood in the Terai and estimates of the likely demand for fuelwood in Nepal until A.D. 2000

The Terai consists of a well-wooded, lightly populated, flat area of the Gangetic plain on the Nepalese side of the border between Nepal and India (see Fig. 7.1). The Government of Nepal has been encouraging the settlement of this region by people from the over-populated, eroded hills and mountains to the north of the country. The pattern of present land-use in Bardia district and the Terai is shown in Table A. 1. The settlement schemes present problems in planning for the future fuel requirements for the people, and these are dealt with in Chapter 7. The discussion in this appendix is confined to the estimates of present fuelwood consumption in the country, and forecasts of requirements to A.D. 2000, assuming that demand can be matched by supply.

The most commonly found timber species is *Shorea robusta* (see Table A. 2). It is rather slow growing and at 80 years can be expected to have a breast height diameter of 50 centimetres: by contrast, *Bombax malabaricum* at 40 years can be expected to reach a diameter of 75 centimetres at breast height. The forests of the Terai have been renowned for the production of high-grade *Shorea* timber which is mostly exported to India as round logs. Exotic species, for example, *Eucalyptus tereticornis*, and *Tectona grandis* are capable of very fast growth but so far comparatively little planting has been undertaken.

TABLE A.1
Land-use in the Terai 1970

Land-use class	Terai[1] Area (thousand ha)	(%)	Bardia Forest Division[2] Area (thousand ha)	(%)
Forest	1781·7	53·6	95·5	60·0
Crops	1263·8	38·0	45·4	28·5
Grassland	91·5	2·8	8·6	5·4
Villages	32·4	1·0	0·9	0·6
Barren	150·5	4·5	8·7	5·5
Barron	4·1	0·1	0·1	—
Other	0·2		—	—
Totals	3324·2	100·0	159·2	100·0

Source: [1] King (1970); [2] Bardia Management Plan.

TABLE A.2

Composition of the natural forests of the Bardia Forest Division, Nepal

Botanical name	Common name	%
Shorea robusta	Sal	53·6
Terminalia tomentosa	Asna	20·6
Bombax malabaricum	Semal	2·8
Dalbergia sissoo	Sissoo	1·8
Acacia Catechu	Khair	1·8
Other species		19·4

TABLE A.3

Population census 1970–72 in Bardia District

Year	Villages	Houses	Population	% growth
1970	514	13 231	91 442	4·4
1971	521	13 625	95 472	9·3
1972	528	14 667	104 428	
			Average 1970–72 = 7·1%	

Source: Malaria Eradication Organization, Malaria Office, Nepalganj.

TABLE A.4

The distribution of population by ethnic origin and family size in Bardia District (1972)

Ethnic origin	Population	% total	Average family size	No. of families
Tharu	41 772	40	13	3210
Hill	5 221	5	6	870
Indian	57 435	55	5	11 487
Total	104 428	100	7	15 567

Source: Malaria Eradication Organization, Malaria Office, Nepalganj.

The population in Bardia is increasing rapidly (Table A.3), mainly as a result of immigration from India and the hills. The settlement of hill people in the Terai is encouraged as part of the policy of the Government of Nepal. Census information on ethnic origin and family size was available at District headquarters (Table A.4) and shows clearly that the indigenous Tharu people live in much larger family units than those of the other ethnic groups and this has an important bearing upon fuel consumption.

Fuelwood is normally carried to households in bullock carts. A survey of the number of cart-loads used per household of each ethnic group per annum was made by Butkas (unpublished 1972), who interviewed 135 families (60 Tharu, 28 Hill, and 47 Indian). The author carried out check surveys in 1973 of 27 families

(11 Tharu and 16 Hill) which confirmed the findings of Butkas, Table A.5. Test weighing of the wood on bullock carts by Butkas and the writer averaged 450 and 675 kilograms respectively. The Forest Department estimate of 560 kilograms per cart has been used in the calculations as it falls almost exactly between the figures obtained in the two surveys.

TABLE A.5

Estimated annual consumption of wood per family: Bardia District (1972)

Ethnic group	Wood (Number of cart-loads)
Tharu	19
Hill	12
Indian	9

Source: Butkas (unpublished 1972)

TABLE A.6

Calculation of annual total and per capita *consumption of fuelwood: Bardia District* (1972)

Ethnic group	Cartloads X families	Total cartloads	Total tonnes	Total m^3	m^3 per capita
Tharu	19 X 3210	60 990	34 154	45 539	1·09
Hill	12 X 870	10 440	5846	7795	1·49
Indian	9 X 11 487	103 383	57 894	77 192	1·34
Totals and mean		174 813	97 895	130 526	1·25

TABLE A.7

Summary of results of various estimates made of fuelwood consumption of Nepalese people

Estimated by	Year	Per capita m^3	Remarks
Clark	1970	0·20	Average for Nepal based on consumption figures for India
Sinden	1971	2·55	Tharu village in Bardia
Butkas	1972	1·09	Tharu villages in Bardia
		1·49	Hill people living in Bardia
		1·34	Indian immigrants in Bardia
Earl	1973	0·85	Tharu village in Bardia
		0·95	Tharu random sample in Bardia
		0·52	Hill people in hills
F.A.O. Yearbook	1970	0·57	Nation-wide based on Forest Department returns

Table A.6 shows clearly that although the indigenous Tharu people use more wood per family, because of their large family size, considerable economies of scale are made and their *per capita* consumption is lower than that of immigrants.

In 1973 the writer carried out a survey of 16 hill families living in the hills and ranging in size from 2—9 members. It was calculated from the survey that the fuelwood consumption was much lower in the areas of scarcity and high price i.e. 0·52 cubic metres *per capita*. A comparative study of the various surveys is made in Table A.7.

It is estimated that the present annual *per capita* fuelwood consumption is about 1·0 cubic metres in the Terai and 0·5 cubic metres elsewhere, or about 0·68 cubic metres for the country as a whole. The F.A.O. figure of 0·57 cubic metres *per capita* appears to be reasonable for overall recorded consumption only. However, because of the migration of people from the forest-denuded north to the forested south, *per capita* consumption in the Terai is likely to decrease as the forest is destroyed and fuel becomes scarcer, but aggregate consumption for the country as a whole is likely to rise dramatically (see Table A.8). Factors likely to

TABLE A.8

Estimated fuelwood requirements Nepal to year 2000 (population in millions, total fuelwood in millions m^3)

	Population	Fuelwood total	Fuelwood m^3 *per capita*
1970			
Terai	4·0	4·0	1·00
Hills and mountains	7·0	3·5	0·50
Totals	11·0	7·5	0·68
1980			
Terai	6·2	5·0	0·80
Hills and mountains	7·4	3·7	0·50
Totals	13·6	8·7	0·64
1990			
Terai	8·7	5·2	0·60
Hills and mountains	8·2	4·1	0·50
Totals	16·9	9·3	0·55
2000			
Terai	11·1	5·6	0·50
Hills and mountains	9·5	4·8	0·50
Totals	20·6	10·4	0·50

Estimated population growth rates (per cent)

	1970—80	1980—90	1990—2000
Terai	4½	3½	2½
Hills	½	1	1½

Average population growth rate for country = 2 per cent

affect demand are population growth, urbanization, and substitution. The price of fuelwood will rise as its marginal utility increases, this will tend to damp down demand at the expense of the poorest members of the community. Table A.8 shows that even allowing for a decrease in *per capita* consumption, the total consumption of fuelwood is likely to rise from 7·5 million cubic metres in 1970 to 10·4 million cubic metres in 2000. The full impact of the fuel shortage, now felt over most of the country, will be as severe in the Terai in 10 years unless preparations to meet it are made soon.

Appendix 2: Fuelwood in Uganda

A calculation of the costs of growing Eucalyptus fuelwood in Uganda

The trees are grown from seed in 15 centimetres long tubes of 8-centimetre lay-flat 150-gauge polythene. They are protected against termite attack by watering with 'Kynadrin' 6 weeks and 1 week before planting in the field. Planting espacement is 2·1 × 2·1 metres (personal communication Watt, A. 1969). The establishment costs per hectare of plantation are shown in Table A.9.

TABLE A.9
*The costs of establishing and maintaining a
Eucalyptus plantation*

Operations 1st year	Costs/ha man-days	
Plants (including tubing, fertilizers, insecticides and transport)	49	
Ground preparation	30	
Lining-out and pitting	25	
Planting	20	
Tending by clean hoeing	49	
Establishment costs	173 ≡	(U.S.$125)[†]
Operations subsequent years		
Annual maintenance	4 ≡	(U.S.$2·88)[†]

[†] Wage rate U.S.$0·72 per man day

The trees grow for 5 or 6 years before harvesting. The second and third crops grow from coppice from the stumps. The difference in rotation makes a difference to the final costs because of the effects of compound interest, here taken as 10 per cent (see Table A.10).

Calculation of costs per unit of wood produced

The yield of fuelwood from *Eucalyptus grandis* on a medium site would be approximately 276 stères at 5 years, and 315 stères at 6 years (site index 30, Kingston 1972) i.e.

$\frac{299}{276} = 1·1$ man-days per stère for the 5 year rotation ≡ U.S.$0·79, and

$\frac{383}{315} = 1·2$ man-days per stère for the 6 year rotation ≡ U.S.$0·86.

Reduction of establishment costs

Agricultural crops, for example, groundnuts, grown between the trees during the first year of the life of the plantation (*taungya* system) would materially reduce the final cost per unit of fuelwood, as shown in the following examples.

		Man-days/ha
Expenses { seed, preparation, and fertilizer weeding, spraying, and harvesting		151
Sale of 1700 kg groundnuts, U.S.$0·11 per kg		260
Net profit from *taungya* operations		109 ≡ U.S.$78

The effect of this reduction in establishment costs on the compounded costs of production of the first crop of fuel would be to reduce this to 124 man-days from 299 man-days for the 5 year rotation and to 190 man-days from 383 man-days for the 6-year rotation. The net growing costs per stère would be reduced from 0·79 to 0·29 U.S.$ and from 0·86 to 0·43 U.S.$ for the 5-year and 6-year rotation respectively.

TABLE A.10

The costs of establishing and maintaining a Eucalyptus plantation

5-year rotation Costs compounded to 5th year at 10%	Costs/ha (man-days)	
173 X 1·610	278·5	
4 X 1·464	5·9	
4 X 1·331	5·3	
4 X 1·210	4·8	
4 X 1·100	4·4	
Total costs for 5-year rotation	298·9	≡ (U.S.$215)
6-year rotation (drier areas) Costs compounded to 6th year at 10%		
173 X 1·772	356·5	
4 X 1·610	6·4	
4 X 1·464	5·9	
4 X 1·331	5·3	
4 X 1·210	4·8	
4 X 1·100	4·4	
Total costs for 6-year rotation	383·3	≡ (U.S.$276)

Table A.11 summarizes the main factors affecting the costs of growing fuelwood plantations in Uganda. The main points to note with reference to the calculations summarized in Table A.11 are: (*a*) although the expected volume increment betwee the 5th and 6th year is 14 per cent, the cost increase, with a 10 per cent rate of interest is even bigger thus producing diminishing returns on capital. If land is not limiting, it would pay to increase the area under plantations and to harvest on a 5-year rotation; (*b*) production costs can be reduced to less than half by *taungya* cultivation in the first year.

TABLE A.11

Growing costs of fuelwood in Uganda in man/days with and without taungya
(10 *per cent interest rate*)

Rotation years	Without *taungya*			With *taungya*		
	Establishment costs per ha	Total costs per ha	Growing costs per stère	Establishment costs per ha	Total costs per ha	Growing costs per stère
5	173	299	1·1	64	125	0·5
6	173	383	1·2	64	190	0·6

Bibliography

Averitt, P. (1961). Coal reserves of the United States and of the world. In *Energy sources* p. 37. National Academy of Sciences. National Research Council, Washington (1962).

Barber, W. (1970). Dualism revisited: economic structures and the framework of economic policy in a post-colonial setting.
In *Unfashionable economics* (ed. P. Streeten), pp. 33–55. Weidenfeld and Nicolson, London.

Beckerman, W. (1972a). Environmental policy: the contribution of economics. *O.E.C.D. Observer* **60**, 34–6.

—— (1972b). Economists, scientists, and environmental catastrophe. *Oxford Economic Papers* **24**, 227–344.

Becking, J. H. (1962). Potential and actual productivity of stem wood in forestry. *Neth. J. agric. Sci.,* **10**, 354–60.

Chapman, P. (1973). No overdrafts in the energy economy. *New Scient.* **58**, 408–10.

Clark, W. P. (1970). *Timber supply and demand 1970–1990* (Nepal project report No. 1). (Mimeographed.) F.A.O., Rome.

Earl, D. E. (1968). Latest techniques in the treatment of natural high forest in South Mengo District. *Paper, 9th commonwealth forestry conference.* Government Printer, Entebbe.

—— Mabonga-Mwisaka, J. (1969). Report of Uganda fellows' visits to the charcoal industry in the U.S.A. and Brazil. *Technical Note 162/70.* Uganda Forest Department, Entebbe.

—— (1970). The Mark V portable steel kiln. *Technical Note 164/70.* Uganda Forest Department, Entebbe.

——(1971). Madagascar—the potential for charcoal. *UNDP FO SF/MAG 8.* F.A.O., Rome.

—— (1972a). Ivory Coast—the place of charcoal in the economy. F.A.O./I.L.O., Abidjan. (Limited circulation.)

—— (1972b). Does forestry need a new ethos? *Paper, 7th world forestry congress.* (Published in *Comm. For. Rev.* **52** (No. 151), 82–9).

—— (1973a). Charcoal and forest management. (Limited circulation.) Department of Forestry, University of Oxford. (A new edition in English, French and Spanish is to be published by F.A.O., Rome.)

—— (1973b). Nepal—the charcoal industry and its potential contribution to the economy of Nepal. Technical Report Nep/69/513. F.A.O., Rome.

F.A.O. (1966a). *World forest inventory 1963.* F.A.O., Rome.

—— (1966b). Wood: world trends and prospects. *Unasylva* **20**.

—— (1970a). *Yearbook of forest products 1969.* F.A.O., Rome.

—— (1970b). *Provisional indicative world plan for agricultural development,* vol, 1. F.A.O., Rome.

—— (1971). *Agricultural commodity projections 1970–1980,* vol. 1. F.A.O., Rome.

—— (1972). *Yearbook of forest products 1970.* F.A.O., Rome.

——(1974). *Yearbook of forest products 1972.* F.A.O., Rome.

Galbraith, J. K. (1969). *The affluent society.* Houghton Mifflin Company, Boston.

Gane, M. (1966). The valuation of growing stock changes. *Q. Jl For.* **60**, 110–20.

Grayson, A. J. (1972). Wood resource and supply potential. *Wd Wood* **13**, 8–9.

Helmers, H. and Bonner, J. (1959). Photosynthetic limits of forest tree yields. *Proceedings of the Society of American Foresters meeting.* pp. 32–5.

Hubbert, M. K. (1973). The energy resources of the earth. *Scien. Am.* **224**, 60–70.

I.B.R.D. (1972). *World bank atlas.* I.B.R.D., Washington D.C.

Intertechnology Corporation (1973). *The U.S. energy problem.* Report for the National Science Foundation, U.S.A.

Kernan, H. S. (1968). Preliminary report on forestry in Vietnam. *Working Paper No. 17.* Joint Development Group, Saigon.

King, K. F. S. (1968). Estimating the size of the productive forest estate. *Obeche* **1**, 10–20.

—— (1970). *Forestry and forest industries in Nepal.* (Unpublished mimeograph.) I.B.R.D. report, Washington D.C.

Kingston, B. (1972). Growth yield and rotation of seedling crops of *Eucalyptus grandis* in Uganda. *Technical Note 193/72.* Uganda Forest Department, Entebbe.

Kira, T. (1969). Promary productivity of tropical rain forest. *Malay. Forester* **32**, 375–84.

—— Ogawa, H., and Yoda, K. (1957). Some unsolved problems in tropical forest ecology. *Proc. Pacif. Sci. congr.* **9**, Vol 4, pp.124–34 (Reprinted 1962).

Kissin, I. (1942). Gas producers for motor vehicles and their operation with forest fuels. *Technical Communication No. 1.* Imperial Forestry Bureau, Oxford.

Landsberg, H. (1945). Climatology. In *Handbook of meteorology,* pp. 928–97. McGraw-Hill, New York.

Lerche, C. and Khan, A. S. (1970). *An estimate of timber trends in West Pakistan.* F.A.O., Rome.

Leslie, A. J. (1971). Economic problems in tropical forestry. *FO/Misc/71/24.* F.A.O., Rome

Lieth, H. (1972). Modeling the primary productivity of the world. *Cienc. Cult.,* **24**, 621–5.

Lipton, M. (1970). Farm price stabilization in underdeveloped agriculture: some aspects on income stability and income distribution. In *Unfashionable economics* (ed. P. Streeten), pp. 3–29. Weidenfeld and Nicholson, London.

—— Streeten, P. (1968). Urban bias and rural planning. In *The crisis of Indian planning,* pp. 83–147. Oxford University Press, London.

Little, I. M. D. and Mirlees, J. A. (1969). *Manual of industrial project analysis in developing countries,* vols 1 and 2, Annexe. O.E.C.D., Paris.

—— Scitovsky, T., and Scott, M. (1970). *Industry and trade in some developing countries. A comparative study.* O.E.C.D., Paris.

Locke, G. M. L. (1970). *Census of woodlands 1965–67.* Forestry Commission publication. H.M.S.O., London.

Logan, W. E. M. (1965). Fast-growing tree species for industrial plantations in developing countries. *Unasylva* **19**, 159–67.

MacGregor, J. J. (1972). A critique of criteria sometimes used in judging forest policies. *Paper, 7th world forestry congress.*

Marris, P. (1968). The social barriers to African entrepreneurship. *J. Dev. Stud.* **5**, 29–38.

Meadows, D. H., Meadows, D. L., Randers, J., and Behrens, W. W. (1972). *The limits to growth.* Earth Island Press, London.

Moore, D. (1957). The effects of an expanding economy on the tropical shelterwood system in Trinidad. *Paper, 7th commonwealth forestry conference.* Forest Department, Port of Spain, Trinidad.

Myrdal, G. (1968). *Asian drama.* Penguin Press, London.

—— (1970). The 'soft state' in underdeveloped countries. In *Unfashionable economi.* (ed. P. Streeten), pp. 227—43: Weidenfeld and Nicolson, London.

National Commission on Agriculture. (1972). *Interim report on production forestry man-made forests.* Government of India, New Delhi.

Nowak, K. and Polycarpou, A. (1969). Sociological problems and Asian forestry. *Unasylva* 23, 19.

O.D.A. (1972). *A guide to project appraisal in developing countries.* H.M.S.O., London.

Olson, J. S. (1970). Carbon cycles and temperate woodlands. *Ecological studies* (ed. D. E. Reichle), pp. 226—41. Chapman & Hall, London.

Openshaw, K. (1971). Present consumption and future requirements of wood in Tanzania. Technical Report 3. *FO SF/Tan 15.* F.A.O., Rome.

Paterson, S. S. (1956). *The forest area of the world and its potential productivity.* Department of Forestry, Royal University of Göteborg, Göteborg.

Political and economic planning (P.E.P.). (1955). *World population and resources.* P.E.P., London.

Reynolds, R. V. and Pierson, A. H. (1942). Fuelwood used in the United States 1630—1930. *U.S.D.A. Circular No. 641.* U.S.D.A., Washington DC.

Roberts, R. (1973). Energy sources and conversion techniques. *Am. Scient.* 61, 66—75.

Rodin, L. E. and Basilevic, N. I. (1967). *Production and mineral cycling in terrestrial vegetation* (translated by G. E. Fogg). Oliver & Boyd, Edinburgh and London.

Runeberg, L. (1972). Wood and plastics: a general review. *Timb. Bull. Eur.* 24, Supplement 5, Vol. 1, 55—66.

Stewart, F. (1972). Technology and employment in less developed countries. Institute of Commonwealth Studies, London. (Mimeographed—limited circulation.)

—— Streeten P, (1973). Conflicts between outputs and employment objectives in developing countries. *Bangladesh Econ. Rev.* 1, 1—24.

Streeten, P. (1967). The frontiers of development studies—some issues of development policy. 4, 2—24.

—— (1972). Technology gaps between rich and poor countries. *Scott. J. polit. Econ.* 19, 213—30.

Sukachev, V. and Dylis, N. (1964). *Fundamentals of forest biogeocoenology* (Translated by J. M. MacLennan (1968)). Oliver & Boyd, Edinburgh and London.

Sutton, W. R. J. (1973). The importance of size and scale in forestry and the forest industries. *N. Z. Jl For.* 18, 63—80.

Troup, R. S. (1926). *A manual of forest mensuration* (Revised ed by C. E. Simmons Government of India, Calcutta.

T.T.K.C. (1962). *Turkiyede yakit problemi ve hal careleri.* Turkiye Tabiatini Koruma Cemiyeti Yayinlari, Ankara.

Uhart, E. (1971). *La forêt amazonienne—source d'energie.* Centre Technique Forestier Tropical, Paris.

U.S.D.A. (1961). Charcoal, production, marketing and use. *Forest Products Researc Laboratory Report No. 2213.* Madison, Wisconsin.

U.N. (1969). *Statistical yearbook 1968.* U.N., New York.

—— (1971). *Statistical yearbook 1970.* U.N., New York.

—— (1973). *Statistical yearbook 1971.* U.N., New York.

Wardle, P. A. (1964). Management and operational research: a linear programming study. *Report on forest research,* pp. 200–10. H.M.S.O., London.

Warman, H. R. (1971). Future problems in petroleum exploration. *Petrol. Rev.* 25, 96–101.

Watt, G. R. (1972). The planning and evaluation of forestry projects. *Institute Paper, No. 45.* Commonwealth Forestry Institue, Oxford.

Webster, G. (1961). *Working plan for South Mengo Forests.* Uganda Forest Department, Entebbe.

Weck, J. (1957). Neure Versuche Zum Problem Der Korrelation: Klina Und Forstliches Produktions Potential. *Forstarchiv* 28, 223–7.

Westoby, J. C. (1963). The role of forest industries in the attack on economic underdevelopment. *Unasylva* 16, 168–201.

Wyatt Smith, J. (1968). Determination of cutting period for THF in Nigeria. *Obeche* 1, 36–48.

Wycherley, P. R. and Templeton, J. K. (1969). Productivity of tropical rain forest. *Malay. Forester* 32, 385.

Yashenko, A. V. (1971). *Use of charcoal tar in highway construction.* Institute of Mechanical Engineers, U.S.S.R.

Abbreviations, Conversion Factors, and Glossary

cal	calorie	Quantity of heat required to raise the temperature of 1 g of water through 1 °C. 1 cal = 4·19 joules.
kcal	kilocalorie	Quantity of heat required to raise the temperature of 1 kg of water through 1°C. 1 kcal = 4190 joules.
CE	coal equivalent	Energy equivalent of 1 tonne of coal. 1 CE $\simeq$ 6·9 × 10^6 kcal $\simeq$ 5·6 barrels of oil $\simeq$ 8000 kWh $\simeq$ 2·3 m^3 fuelwood (dry)
	cord	128 cubic feet stacked wood $\simeq$ 2·12 m^3 solid wood.
CV	Calorific value	The number of kcal given out when 1 g of a substance is completely burnt. Calorific value of fuels mentioned in this book: Paraffin 10·4 fuel oil 9·8 charcoal 7·1 coal 6·9 wood (oven dry) 4·7 cow dung (dry) 4·0 peat (dry) 4·0 wood (air dry) 20–30% m.c. 3·5
	Entropy Law	The entropy of the universe at all times moves towards a maximum. Most familiar as the Second Law of Thermodynamics.
	enrichment	Planting trees in the gaps of a refined forest in order that they may form a useful part of the future crop.
	fuelwood factors	1 cart (a) 2 bullock $\simeq$ 560 kg (air dry) 1 cart (b) 4 bullock $\simeq$ 938 kg (air dry) 1 cord = 128 ft^3 (stacked) = 2·12 m^3 (solid) 1 headload $\simeq$ 37 kg (Nepal, air dry) 1 m^3 = 725 kg (general), 750 (non-coniferous) 1 stère = 1 m^3 stacked 1 tonne = 1·38 m^3 (general), 1·33 (non-coniferous) 1 large lorry load $\simeq$ 10 tonnes (India) 1 small lorry load $\simeq$ 5 tonnes (Nepal).
GDP	gross domestic product	The value of the total flow of goods produced by a national economy.

GNP	gross national product	As for GDP plus net income from investment abroad.
ha	hectare	2·471 acres
inc	increment	The amount of wood added to a tree or forest during a defined period.
IRR	internal rate of return	The rate of return that is being earned on capital tied up, while it is tied up, after allowing for recoupment of the initial investment.
j	joule	Unit of work. 4·19 joules = 1 calorie
kj	kilojoule	1000 joules
kWh	kilowatt-hour	= 1 unit = the quantity of energy furnished in one hour by a current whose power or rate of expenditure of energy is a kilowatt. 1 kWh = 864 kcal. 1000 kWh = 0·125 tonnes CE
m^3	cubic metre	= 35·31 ft^3
m.c.	moisture content	For wood and charcoal $$m.c. = \frac{(\text{weight fresh} - \text{weight.oven dry}) \times 100}{\text{weight oven dry}}$$
	marginal investment rate	The opportunity-cost rate of return for government, sometimes termed the cut-off rate.
NDR	net discounted revenue	The present value of future revenues when discounted costs are subtracted from discounted revenues at a given rate of interest.
P	power	Rate of energy flow measured in watts.
	refining	Cleaning and thinning natural forests with the object of increasing the proportion of potential final crop timber trees.
s.g.	specific gravity	
	stère	1 stacked m^3
	taungya	A system of establishing forest plantations whereby agricultural crops are grown between the newly planted trees until the canopy is closed.
THF	tropical high forest	
TSI	timber stand improvement	
W	watt	

Index

Acacia, 27
Acacia catechu, 111
acetic acid, 26, 29, 33, 34
acetone, 33, 34
Africa, 5, 12, 47, 54, 57, 59, 60, 62
africanization, 5
agricultural
    crops, 39
    energy, 15
    wastes, 18, 20, 60
aid, 6, 107
    bi-lateral, 108, 109
    multi-lateral, 108, 109
Algeria, 10
Alnus rubra, 24
Amazon, 37
amenity values, 107
Argentina, 31, 56
Asia, 54, 59, 83
    Pacific, 55, 60, 62
Australia, 31, 34

Bangladesh, 18
bark, 53
Belgium 7, 10
blast furnace, 99
boats, 26
Bombax malabaricum, 110, 111
bone charcoal, 28
Bosch process, 35
Brazil, 7, 10, 31, 56, 60, 105
brick works, 26
butane, 68, 70

calorific value, 22, 24
    gross, 22, 23
    net, 22
Canada, 7, 10, 24, 60
carbon
    dioxide, 26, 34, 35, 38
    fixation, land, 40–1
    monoxide, 26, 34, 35, 69
    net primary production of, 38, 39
carbonization, 26, 28, 72
    systems, 30
    techniques, 28
cement, 31
Central African Republic, 105, 106

charcoal, 20, 22, 23, 24, 26, 27, 34, 36, 50,
    51, 52, 54, 60, 68, 69, 70, 72
    activated, 27, 32, 57, 80, 89
    ash content, 27
    briquettes, 32, 53, 54, 80, 89
    calorific value, 27
    coconut shell, 28, 33, 35
    consumption, 58
    consumption, world, 56
    cost of, 72, 73, 74, 75
    domestic, 30
    exports, 57, 67, 89
    fixed carbon, 27
    for cement manufacture, 28
    hardness, 27
    industrial, 27, 31
    industries, 85
    iron and steelworks, 31, 99
    moisture content, 27
    nature and properties, of 27
    phosophorus content, 27
    production, world, 19
    pulverized fuel, 31, 67
    raw materials for, 28
    sewage filters, 31
    specific gravity, 24, 27
    specific surface area, 27
    stability, 27
    sulphur content, 27
    transport cost, 74, 75
    value added, 32
    volatile matter, 27
    water purification, 31
Chile, 7, 10
coal, 14, 16, 17, 19, 20, 21, 22, 24, 60, 69,
    70
    equivalent, 6, 10, 12, 53, 105
reserves, 16, 17, 18
specific gravity, 24
coke, 69
combustion, 23
compound interest, 48
conifers, 23
consumer preference, 60, 61, 74
copper, 103
coppice with standards, 36, 52
cost-benefit analysis, 51, 76
cow dung, 18, 63

fuelwood *cont.*
  elasticity of demand, 66
  exports, 80
  price of, 68, 69, 70, 71
  production, world, 19
  requirement *per capita,* 88
  stacked, 25
  transport cost, 74, 75
furnace, Herreschoff, 29
furnaces, 28, 30

gas, 14
gene bank, 49
geothermal, 6, 15, 19, 20, 104
Germany, 57
Ghana, 57
GNP, 1, 3, 4, 6, 7, 50, 59, 64, 65, 82, 88, 102
  per capita, 2, 3, 4, 7, 10, 58, 60, 64, 65, 106
gravitational energy, 13, 14, 15
Greece, 7, 10, 60
Guinea, 10

hand-made paper, 26
hot springs, 14
hydro-electric energy, 6, 15, 19, 20, 21, 64, 101, 103, 104
hydrogen, 23, 26, 35, 36, 69
hydrological cycle, 14

import substitution, 6
India, 2, 4, 10, 18, 31, 35, 60, 63, 68, 69, 70, 99–100, 105, 110
indicated reserves, 15, 16
indirect benefits, 78
inferred reserves, 15, 16
intangible benefits, 80
interior energy, 12, 14, 15
internal combustion engine, 35, 36
iron ore, 80
Italy, 7, 10, 60
Ivory Coast, 7, 10, 72, 100, 101, 105, 106

jaggeries, 26
Japan, 28, 56–7

Kenya, 5, 10, 35, 57, 68
kilns, 26, 30
  brick, 29
  concrete, 29
  continuous, 28, 29, 30
  earth, 29, 73, 79
  pit, 29
  portable, 73
  portable steel, 28, 29, 100

Lacotte process, 37
land settlement, 94, 96, 98, 99
  schemes, 84
Latin America, 54, 55, 59, 60, 62
Libya, 7, 10
linear programming, 90
linkage effects, 80, 84
long-wave thermal radiation, 14

Madagascar, 10, 72, 100, 101, 105, 106
Maesopsis eminii, 24, 33
Malawi, 10
Malaysia, 31, 56
marginal cost of capital, 91
marginal investment rate, 82
market economies, 61, 75
measured reserves, 15, 16
Mengo system, 71, 90
methane, 26
methyl alchohol (methanol) 19, 23, 26, 29, 33, 34, 35, 54, 69
monocultures, 107

natural forests, 39, 47, 48, 49, 107
natural gas, 16, 17, 20, 21
natural gas reserves, 18
NDR, 90, 108
Nepal, 6, 7, 10, 18, 57, 58, 60, 63, 64, 66, 68, 69, 70, 72, 73, 74, 82, 92, 94–9, 100, 101, 105, 106, 110–4
Nigeria, 10
nitrogen, 26, 34, 35
North America, 54, 55, 60, 62
nuclear
  energy, 15, 16, 17
  fission, 17, 21, 104
  fuel, 103
  fusion, 17, 21, 104
  power, 6, 103

Oak, She, 99
Oak, Silky, 99
oil, 14, 16, 17, 20, 21, 24, 103
  from coal, 103
  fuel, 22, 68, 69, 70
    specific gravity, 24
  reserves, 18
  shale, 16, 17, 103
  tar sands, 16, 17, 103
opportunity costs, 48, 49, 52, 79, 81, 91, 105, 107

Pakistan, 18
paraffin, 22, 24, 68, 69, 70
paraffin, specific gravity, 24
Paterson's index, 42
peat, 22